MW01485881

"STATON" THE FACTS
THE INFORMATIVE
BIBLE BASED ACTIVITY BOOK

CONTENTS

Scriptures taken from the New King James Version of the Bible. Copyright 1982 by Thomas Nelson, Inc. Used by permission. All rights reserved.

WORD SCRAMBLE

WORD SCRAMBLE – SHEET #1

NOAH'S ARK

The words below are associated with the story of Noah, God's faithful servant. Noah receives the command to build in Genesis Chapter 6 and steps out of the ark onto dry land at the end of Chapter 8.

1. HAON   _____

2. SLAMIAN   _____

3. OFLOD   _____

4. RAWET   _____

5. NAIR   _____

6. EODV   _____

7. NEVAR   _____

8. LBMAS   _____

9. STNPHALEE   _____

10. OSINL   _____

11. SEFFAIGR   _____

12. ETBEDION   _____

13. LDBUI   _____

14. YFOTR   _____

15. AYLMIF   _____

FUN FACT: There are three arks mentioned in the Old Testament: Noah's Ark (made of gopher wood), Moses' Ark (made of bulrushes), and the Ark of the Covenant (made of shittim wood).

WORD SCRAMBLE – SHEET #2

A CHILD IS BORN

"But you, Bethlehem, in the land of Judah, are not the least among the rulers of Judah; For out of you shall come a Ruler who will shepherd My people Israel." (Matthew 2:6)

1. YARM _____

2. PHOSEJ _____

3. SJESU _____

4. EWSENIM _____

5. PERSHDHE _____

6. GREMAN _____

7. LEHEMTHEB _____

8. MIGA _____

9. STIFG _____

10. NIGRVI _____

11. THIRB _____

12. TARS _____

13. EPOH _____

14. YOJ _____

15. CEAPE _____

FUN FACT: The Ark of the Covenant symbolizes the presence of God.

WORD SCRAMBLE – SHEET #3

JOB

MEANING OF NAME: "ONE PERSECUTED"

In the Book of Job, we see a man of great wealth and many resources lose everything. He lost his property, possessions, even his children. Though he was besieged with grief, he never gave up on God. Strong was his faith and trust in the Lord. As children of the Most High God, we also must have strong faith.

1. ZLIPHAE _____

2. ROZPHA _____

3. DABIDL _____

4. TCFEPRE _____

5. FUTHLAIF _____

6. REFFUS _____

7. ISTROGEHU _____

8. NATAS _____

9. RIEDSFN _____

10. TNERPE _____

11. AHVOEJH _____

12. THYLEAW _____

13. YALOL _____

14. TSUTR _____

15. NOITATMEPT _____

FUN FACT: King Solomon had 700 wives, princesses, and 300 concubines.

WORD SCRAMBLE – SHEET #4

THE WEDDING PARTY IN CANA

In the Book of John at the wedding in Cana of Galilee Jesus performs His first miracle by turning water into the very best wine the host ever had. No one except Christ's mother Mary and His disciples knew where that tasty wine had come from.

1. DWINGED   _____

2. RAWET   _____

3. YRAM   _____

4. SJEUS   _____

5. NEWI   _____

6. STPORTEAW   _____

7. DEBIR   _____

8. MOGRO   _____

9. SEBT   _____

10. ODOG   _____

11. GLIEEAL   _____

12. DOOF   _____

13. GAPRES   _____

14. MRTHOE   _____

15. SIPELDCIS   _____

FUN FACT: King Solomon had 1,400 chariots and 12, 000 horsemen.

WORD SCRAMBLE – SHEET #5

THE LION'S DEN

In the 6th chapter of the Book of Daniel, Daniel defies a decree enacted by king Darius. Because he disobeyed the decree he was cast into a den of lions. The next day he was discovered unharmed. Almighty God had shut the lions' mouths. God is faithful, merciful, loving, and kind. He protects they who put their trust in Him and obey His commands.

1. NELIAD _____

2. LREDACNEVIE _____

3. NYETNI _____

4. SOLIN _____

5. WPFULERO _____

6. YPTIVCAIT _____

7. ROHON _____

8. PRIEME _____

9. ODG _____

10. EDN _____

11. VERBA _____

12. TROGSN _____

13. ROTECPT _____

14. FEAS _____

15. DFEATE _____

FUN FACT: King Solomon spoke 3,000 proverbs and 1,005 songs.

WORD SCRAMBLE – SHEET #6

GOD'S GRACE

"For sin shall not have dominion over you, for you are not under law but under grace." (Romans 6:14) (NKJV)

1. CRAGE   _____
2. UDABON   _____
3. VELO   _____
4. CYERM   _____
5. SLEGIBSN   _____
6. ELSAIR   _____
7. NTEPER   _____
8. SHIMSEA   _____
9. OVEFRIG   _____
10. AELH   _____
11. DRSLCEKSIBA _____
12. TIENFFUSCI _____
13. LAGHTYMI   _____
14. RAFOV   _____
15. NESSOOGD   _____

FUN FACT: The agreement God and the Israelites made at Mount Sinai is called the Law Covenant.

WORD SCRAMBLE – SHEET #7

DAVID AND GOLIATH

In 1 Samuel Chapter 17 we find the story of a brave, shepherd boy, David, who defeated a Philistine giant named Goliath. Goliath, who stood over nine feet tall, was defeated by the fearless child with a sling and stone.

1. TAIGN _____

2. HDSEPRHE _____

3. TSSOHIGNL _____

4. ENTOS _____

5. DIAVD _____

6. TOGLIHA _____

7. VABRE _____

8. MPONIHCA _____

9. OCATMB _____

10. ITNEPIHLIS _____

11. TLAL _____

12. TYMIGH _____

13. LAUS _____

14. GKNI _____

15. RIORWAR _____

FUN FACT: Esther's cousin Mordecai raised her as if she was his own daughter. Her biological father's name was Abihail.

WORD SCRAMBLE – SHEET #8

DAY OF THE LORD

16 For the Lord Himself will descend from heaven with a shout, with the voice of an archangel, and with the trumpet of God. And the dead in Christ will rise first. **17** Then we who are alive and remain shall be caught up together with them in the clouds to meet the Lord in the air. And thus we shall always be with the Lord. **18** Therefore comfort one another with these words. (1 Thessalonians 4:16-18) (NKJV)

1. MNJDUGTE _____

2. GOYLR _____

3. DOG _____

4. ONIZ _____

5. THISCR _____

6. REDIVLE _____

7. GLESNIBS _____

8. REOESTR _____

9. MOIDGKN _____

10. GNVERSAELTI _____

11. ROSEINGVE _____

12. CLUDO _____

13. HAVEEN _____

14. WEN JREUMSALE _____

FUN FACT: The color purple typifies Christ as the sovereign one; the King of kings and Lord of lords.

WORD SCRAMBLE – SHEET #9

NAMES ASSOCIATED WITH CHRIST

There is a plethora of names associated with our Blessed Savior. Below are popular names noted in scripture.

1. CHABRN _____

2. SEJUS _____

3. VOIRSA _____

4. DLOR _____

5. CUOESLNOR _____

6. RETCHAE _____

7. PHTPROE _____

8. JGDUE _____

9. RDOW _____

10. EREDMERE _____

11. HSSMEIA _____

12. UERT NEIV _____

13. YDA RINSPG _____

14. DOCAVTEA _____

15. MBAL _____

FUN FACT: Scarlet red is the sacrificial color. It embodies the entire thought of redemption.

WORD SCRAMBLE – SHEET #10

NAMES ASSOCIATED WITH CHRIST

Below are names associated with our Blessed Savior.

1. JAHEHVO   _____

2. EONUWLRFD   _____

3. SHLIOH   _____

4. NSO   _____

5. NEAZERNA   _____

6. NOINMGR ATRS   _____

7. IRPCEN FO ECEAP   _____

8. OROT FO VDIAD   _____

9. IGKN FO NKISG   _____

10. YHOL NEO   _____

11. HPAAL NAD GAMOE   _____

12. RDABE FO FELI   _____

13. RROECNEOSTN   _____

14. IRSTF AND LATS   _____

15. SEIRTENVLAG HETFRA   _____

FUN FACT: The color blue is a heavenly color. It typifies Christ as the spiritual one.

WORD SCRAMBLE – SHEET #11

INTO THE FIRE

In the third chapter of the Book of Daniel we read about evil Nebuchadnezzar and his idolatrous ways. He wanted everyone to worship golden images. Three brave Jewish men named Shadrach, Meshach and Abed-Nego refused to obey him. They were cast into a fiery furnace, but four figures were seen walking amidst the flames! God sent an angel into the fire to deliver them from harm. He will do the same for you and me.

1. HADRASCH   _____

2. HESHCMA   _____

3. ONEGBADE   _____

4. WSIEHJ   _____

5. TEERH   _____

6. ENM   _____

7. LNDAEI   _____

8. REFI   _____

9. DGO   _____

10. GINK   _____

11. LNOBYAB   _____

12. FAMELS   _____

13. CRHTIS   _____

14. SELTHREDE   _____

15. UNABLECHUOT   _____

FUN FACT: In the bible, the number forty stands for trials, probations, and testing. It is mentioned in the bible 146 times.

WORD SCRAMBLE – SHEET #12

FRUIT OF THE SPIRIT

In the Book of Galatians Apostle Paul writes to the churches in Galatia. In chapter 5:16-26 he encourages the people of Galatia to Walk in the Spirit. Paul tells them not to fulfill the lust of the flesh and provides examples of works of the flesh and the fruit of the spirit.

1. VEOL _____

2. YOJ _____

3. ECAPE _____

4. ATIPECEN _____

5. SNIDEKSN _____

6. DOGESONS _____

7. USLAFINSTHFE _____

8. SNEGTLENES _____

9. NEKSSEEM _____

10. FLES-TLNOCRO _____

11. LAUP _____

12. ESIPLET _____

13. SNIATAALG _____

14. DKNIGOM _____

15. RANTEPECEN _____

FUN FACT: Anointed oil symbolizes the Holy Spirit. The Holy Spirit is our anointed helper.

WORD SCRAMBLE – SHEET #13

ADAM AND EVE

The story of Adam and Eve is about love, temptation, disobedience, and the consequences that come with defying the commands of Almighty God.

1. NACI _____

2. LABE _____

3. THES _____

4. REDRUM _____

5. NIS _____

6. TRUIF _____

7. HEWAHY _____

8. NATAS _____

9. GENRAD _____

10. NEED _____

11. TREPSEN _____

12. DENBIFORD _____

13. DOOG _____

14. LIVE _____

15. KENAD _____

FUN FACT: In the 17th chapter of Genesis God made a covenant with Abram (renamed Abraham). Abraham was designated as the father of many nations.

WORD SCRAMBLE – SHEET #14

ABRAHAM

MEANING OF NAME: "FATHER OF A MULTITUDE"

1. VOCANTEN _____

2. POMISER _____

3. THRAFE _____

4. TANONI _____

5. SHILAME _____

6. ASCIA _____

7. HARAS _____

8. AMRAB _____

9. DORL _____

10. CROTEPT _____

11. AGHRA _____

12. THAIF _____

13. STANDNCESED _____

14. RYTOSHI _____

15. BESLINGS _____

FUN FACT: Abraham's wife Sarai (renamed Sarah) was designated as the mother of nations.

WORD SCRAMBLE – SHEET #15

JACOB/ISRAEL

1. RLCAHE   _____

2. HEAL   _____

3. DAG   _____

4. ITLAHANP   _____

5. MONESI   _____

6. VILE   _____

7. DAJHU   _____

8. RASEH   _____

9. BURENE   _____

10. MANJENIB   _____

11. PHOSJE   _____

12. CHASSRIA   _____

13. BUNZELU   _____

14. NAD   _____

15. NAHDI   _____

FUN FACT: God made a covenant promise to Abraham that He would bless his descendants and give them the land of Canaan. Fourteen years later, Abraham and Sarah were blessed with a son named Isaac.

WORD SCRAMBLE – SHEET #16

BIBLE BOOKS – OT and NT

1. GNEISSE _____

2. RNOITCNSAIH _____

3. UTLVISICE _____

4. OMIHNELP _____

5. YDONRUTOEME _____

6. TNRIEVEOLA _____

7. EJDGSU _____

8. OHIDAAB _____

9. AUSMEL _____

10. TMHYTIO _____

11. LROECHNCIS _____

12. EVRBSPRO _____

13. EMIAHHEN _____

14. SITUT _____

15. BOJ _____

FUN FACT: Jacob, whom God later refers to as Israel, had twelve sons and one daughter via four women (Leah, Rachel, Bilhah, and Zilpah). His sons formed the twelve tribes of Israel.

WORD SCRAMBLE – SHEET #17

BIBLE BOOKS – OT and NT

1. DOSXUE _____

2. AROMNS _____

3. NREMUBS _____

4. EENIHSPAS _____

5. JOASUH _____

6. EWSHBRE _____

7. UTHR _____

8. EMEHRAIJ _____

9. KSNGI _____

10. WTMAHTE _____

11. RAZE _____

12. NEAZHHIAP _____

13. CAHIM _____

14. SMSALP _____

15. KAUHKBKA _____

FUN FACT: Abraham's first son was by Sarah's Egyptian maid servant, Hagar. Ishmael fathered twelve princes: Nebajoth, Kedar, Adbeel, Mibsam, Mishma, Dumah, Massa, Hadar, Tema, Jetur, Naphish, and Kedemah. Ishmael is father of the Arabs.

WORD SCRAMBLE – SHEET #18

BIBLE BOOKS – OT and NT

1. HJNO _____

2. OANHJ _____

3. RPTEE _____

4. AUMNH _____

5. DLAENI _____

6. GAHIAG _____

7. ONRAMS _____

8. CSOOSSIALN _____

9. MCALAHI _____

10. KMRA _____

11. ISIAAH _____

12. LPPPNIIIHSA _____

13. HSEETR _____

14. TLSMOAINTENA _____

15. SNNOSHSAIEALT _____

FUN FACT: Mark wrote the gospel directed to the Romans. The book of Mark has 16 chapters with nearly 700 verses and approximately 15,000 words.

WORD SCRAMBLE – SHEET #19

BIBLE BOOKS – OT and NT

1. HZIAAHECR _____

2. ECSSELICSTEA _____

3. GNOS FO ONSOMLO _____

4. UDJE _____

5. CATS _____

6. KELU _____

7. LOEJ _____

8. SEAOH _____

9. SOMA _____

10. SAMEJ _____

11. ILEZEEK _____

FUN FACT: The name Moses means "to draw". Moses was a Hebrew leader, lawgiver, mediator, and prophet. He is one of the most significant figures in the bible. The story of Moses is mentioned in Exodus, Leviticus, Numbers, and Deuteronomy.

WORD SCRAMBLE – SHEET #20

HOSEA
MEANING OF NAME: "GOD IS HELP"

The Book of Hosea contains two stories. One story is about Hosea and his adulterous wife Gomer. The second story is about the Lord, His people Israel, and blessings that are to come. Below are a few names of individuals found in the Book of Hosea.

1. AOHES _____

2. EBIRE _____

3. AZIHZU _____

4. MTHAJO _____

5. ZAHA _____

6. IEHZAKEH _____

7. OEGRM _____

8. LAMIIDB _____

9. EEJLZRE _____

10. JUHE _____

11. OL- AMUAHHR _____

12. OL-MIMA _____

13. DAIDV _____

14. AMIRPEH _____

15. JHUDA _____

FUN FACT: The name Aaron means "lofty, exalted one". Aaron was the first high priest. As High Priest, he led ceremonies and sacrifices and had the authority to enter the Holy of Holies. To become a High Priest, one must be a direct descendant in the line of Aaron.

WORD SCRAMBLE – SHEET #21

LOCATIONS – BOOK OF AMOS
MEANING OF NAME: "BURDEN OR BURDEN BEARER"

In the Book of Amos, the transgressions of Damascus, Gaza, Tyre, Edom, Ammon, Moab, Judah, and Israel are mentioned along with the judgments of Almighty God. This prophetic book has nine chapters.

1. TEOAK   _____

2. ALCERM   _____

3. SASMCDUA   _____

4. LDIGEA   _____

5. HELZAA   _____

6. RIK   _____

7. GAAZ   _____

8. SDAODH   _____

9. HAELKOSN   _____

10. TREY   _____

11. NORKE   _____

12. MODE   _____

13. RBHOAZ   _____

14. NOMMA   _____

15. MANTE   _____

FUN FACT: Hell is called Hades in Greek and Sheol in Hebrew.

WORD SCRAMBLE – SHEET #22

JONAH

MEANING OF NAME: "DOVE"

The Book of Jonah illustrates God's loving mercy.

1. HONAJ _____

2. VEHNINE _____

3. PAJOP _____

4. SHISHTAR _____

5. TLINAIFFCO _____

6. SWOLLIB _____

7. SWAEV _____

8. HISF _____

9. GORCA _____

10. PHIS _____

11. DALN _____

12. YELLB _____

13. EYCMR _____

14. YRDPAE _____

15. ETLEPM _____

FUN FACT: Psalm 119 is the longest psalm. It contains 22 units of 8 verses each.

WORD SCRAMBLE – SHEET #23

NAMES – BOOK OF MATTHEW
MEANING OF NAME: "GIFT OF THE LORD"

The Book of Matthew has 28 chapters. It opens with the genealogy of Abraham to the birth of Jesus Christ. A total of 42 generations are noted in 17 verses! Matthew, also known as Levi, was a tax collector, a writer, and a Pastor in Damascus.

1. SUSEJ ISTCHR _____

2. VIDDA _____

3. HAMABRA _____

4. ACISA _____

5. OBJAC _____

6. REZPE _____

7. AHZER _____

8. MARTA _____

9. AZBO _____

10. NHONAHS _____

11. EDOB _____

12. SOONLOM _____

13. THRU _____

14. REHAMOBO _____

15. ABHIJA _____

FUN FACT: The longest chapter in the bible is Matthew 26 with 74 verses.

WORD SCRAMBLE – SHEET #24

BOOK OF JOHN

In the very first chapter of the Book of John our Sovereign Savior is referred to as the Word, the True Light, The Lamb of God, The Son of God, The Messiah, Rabbi, and the King of Israel! Every chapter henceforth illustrates why Christ has been regarded as such. John writes about Christ's ministry in the vicinity of Judea, highlighting some of the miracles performed such as walking on water, changing water to wine, healing the blind man, raising the dead, and the forgiveness of sin.

1. ODEMNICUS _____

2. GDOKINM _____

3. SIRIPT _____

4. RODESTY _____

5. MPLTEE _____

6. POVEASSR _____

7. SCRIREPTU _____

8. UILBD _____

9. WBOM _____

10. ORBN _____

11. NDWI _____

12. ACHTEER _____

13. TESYTIF _____

14. EVENAHLY _____

15. CIPLEDISS _____

FUN FACT: The book of John has 21 chapters and 878 verses. Chapter 6 has the most verses (71) and chapters 2 and 21 have the least (25).

WORD SCRAMBLE – SHEET #25

THE ACTS OF THE APOSTLES

The Acts of the Apostles is the fifth New Testament book. Written by Luke, the acts of Apostles Peter, Paul and John are frequently mentioned throughout this 28-chapter book. In chapter 2 Peter preached about the life, death, and resurrection of Jesus Christ on The Day of Pentecost.

1. IONSNAT   _____

2. GERA   _____

3. TILGENES   _____

4. MILERAC   _____

5. YHOL   _____

6. INVA   _____

7. DUCSADEES   _____

8. VANSERT   _____

9. MPSANIONCO   _____

10. BODLO   _____

11. LESAPOST   _____

12. TRIDOCNE   _____

13. PIERST   _____

14. MORINGN   _____

15. RECHILDN   _____

FUN FACT: The rainbow is a symbol of God's covenant with his people.

WORD SCRAMBLE – SHEET #26

THE BOOK OF GALATIANS

The Book of Galatians, written by Apostle Paul, shows us that the believer is no longer under the law, but saved by faith alone. The word faith was noted 19 times (**1** time in chapter 1, **3** times in chapter 2, **14** times in chapter 3, and **2** times in chapter 5). The Book of Galatians consists of 6 chapters, 3,086 words, 149 verses.

1. LENESWDS _____

2. DERMURS _____

3. SORRCEY _____

4. SFLEH _____

5. URDALTYE _____

6. NNOIORCTAIF _____

7. YDRLATOI _____

8. VENY _____

9. THRAW _____

10. RDEATH _____

11. ITIRNHE _____

12. IBNGROEH _____

13. FSFLNUTSAHIE _____

14. OEONSGSD _____

15. SDKSENIN _____

FUN FACT: Sitting in sackcloth and ashes is a symbol of repentance.

WORD SCRAMBLE – SHEET #27
PSALMS

One Hundred and Fifty poignant psalms (songs) make up the amazing Book of Psalms. This book is also known as the Book of Praises. Authorship has been attributed to: King David (75), the sons of Korah (12), Asaph (12), Solomon (2), Ethan the Ezrahite (1), Moses (1) and anonymous authors (47).

1. DLRO _____

2. DERPHESH _____

3. OMFTRCO _____

4. LEYLAV _____

5. FOWOLL _____

6. STAREUPS _____

7. THEAD _____

8. ESENMIE _____

9. VERFORE _____

10. TAONIN _____

11. SOETGSNHIREUS _____

12. SDGEONOS _____

13. DASHOW _____

14. RYCME _____

15. TAFFS _____

FUN FACT: Thunder is a symbol for God's voice.

WORD SCRAMBLE – SHEET #28
PETER FREED FROM PRISON

1. RETEP _____

2. REHOD _____

3. IMRPISNO _____

4. JHNO _____

5. JMEAS _____

6. TRGMANE _____

7. NIVSOI _____

8. ALSSNDA _____

9. WSHEJI _____

10. PATRED _____

11. KRSTCU _____

12. VITCIM _____

13. CKONK _____

14. TEAG _____

15. LIRG _____

FUN FACT: Eight times in the Book of Isaiah the people are asked to "Wait on the Lord".

WORD SCRAMBLE – SHEET #29
MICHAL

The sons of Saul were Jonathan, Jishui, and Malchishua and the names of his daughters were Merab and Michal.

1. DRAGHUET _____

2. SLAU _____

3. NIGK _____

4. ESERMEGSN _____

5. RUGNOEY _____

6. JNONATAH _____

7. VIADD _____

8. RILHW _____

9. BLATET _____

10. TADEH _____

11. CENAD _____

12. SITSER _____

13. NITGHOT _____

14. DOWWIN _____

15. GORNIMN _____

FUN FACT: "The Lord of Hosts" is mentioned 62 times in the Book of Isaiah.

WORD SCRAMBLE – SHEET #30

DINAH

Dinah, is the daughter of Leah and Jacob. Raped by Shechem, her assault was avenged by brothers Levi and Simeon. Shechem, his father Hamor, and every circumcised male in the city were killed. Dinah is mentioned in Genesis 30:1, 34:1, 13, 25, 26.

1. TERSIS _____

2. HELA _____

3. ROTHBER _____

4. EFLIDE _____

5. NDIK _____

6. CHEEMSH _____

7. AMHOR _____

8. ITVIHE _____

9. SINEOM _____

10. LEIV (Name) _____

11. WODSR _____

12. WINDDEG _____

13. YRARM _____

14. UNNOI _____

15. BERID _____

FUN FACT: "The Holy One of Israel" is mentioned 25 times in the Book of Isaiah.

WORD SCRAMBLE – SHEET #31

AMOS

"Burden Bearer"

The Minor Prophet Amos was a sheep breeder and a tender of Sycamore fruit before being called to prophesy. This amazing book is composed of nine amazing chapters with a total of 146 spectacular verses.

1. SLEARFES _____

2. THAFILFU _____

3. BELHUM _____

4. SEWI _____

5. BREWEH _____

6. VABER _____

7. PTEPORH _____

8. ADJUH _____

9. LEARSI _____

10. VECERL _____

11. MEJOBROA _____

12. KOOB _____

13. RMEAFR _____

14. ERREDH _____

15. SSIVINO _____

FUN FACT: The name of the prophet Isaiah means "Salvation is of the Lord" or "The Lord is salvation".

WORD SCRAMBLE – SHEET #32

ORDER OF WORSHIP

1. VOIIOTNNCA   _____

2. EYRRAP   _____

3. MEORNS   _____

4. DNINCIUTTORO   _____

5. NIGOLSC   _____

6. SNGO   _____

7. BGILSNES   _____

8. FNRIFEOG   _____

9. DNEBOITCINE   _____

10. ROSIPWH   _____

11. VSERECI   _____

12. RTEUPCSIR   _____

13. DRANIEG   _____

14. REDOR   _____

15. STYOMNETI   _____

FUN FACT: The name Nehemiah means "Jehovah Has Consoled".

WORD SCRAMBLE – SHEET #33

JEREMIAH

MEANING OF NAME: "THE LORD HURLS"

1. OELWRPUF _____
2. ENOOAMTLI _____
3. NEJGTDUM _____
4. VNAONECT _____
5. OTRPPHE _____
6. ONLOOMS _____
7. EJLUMARSE _____
8. ONIMCOSSIM _____
9. NSIGK _____
10. EOTNUCYRNM _____
11. LEPMTE _____
12. JDAHU _____
13. NBBOYLA _____
14. NNTIOA _____
15. KPSSMANOE _____

FUN FACT: Nehemiah's father's name Hachaliah means "Jehovah Enlightens". Hachaliah was from the tribe of Judah.

WORD SCRAMBLE – SHEET #34

HABAKKUK

MEANING OF NAME: "EMBRACE"

1. LNVIEOCE   _____

2. LFCTNCOI   _____

3. EUIJTSNCI   _____

4. SIIVNNAO   _____

5. UNPISH   _____

6. KIWECD   _____

7. CUFCLSSEUS   _____

8. RVEEEILB   _____

9. AANSIVOLT   _____

10. TGHETSRN   _____

11. RGETSGLU   _____

12. TLBUREO   _____

13. CDSGIRAE   _____

14. OEICJER   _____

15. RLDVEIE   _____

FUN FACT: A prophet is a person who delivers a message directly from God.

WORD SCRAMBLE – SHEET #35

ZEPHANIAH

MEANING OF NAME: "THE LORD HAS HIDDEN"

1. NANENNEOCMTU _____

2. IMSEPRO _____

3. TURUEF _____

4. PERAEENTCN _____

5. SIHOJA _____

6. EVDNII _____

7. NOPACITML _____

8. INEIRPPCL _____

9. SOPIERNOSP _____

10. SGLESNDA _____

11. SIPHUN _____

12. EGJUD _____

13. OEELPP _____

14. IGRNILOE _____

15. VERIVE _____

FUN FACT: Micah predicted the Savior would be born in Bethlehem.

WORD SCRAMBLE – SHEET #36

NAHUM

MEANING OF NAME: "COMPASSIONATE"

1. AFTSSE   _____

2. VSWO   _____

3. EKCDWI   _____

4. NENVEIH   _____

5. GIUYLT   _____

6. LDOOF   _____

7. OSLCEPAL   _____

8. EPALCA   _____

9. TEGA   _____

10. RERIV   _____

11. EYNEM   _____

12. LFLA   _____

13. VSRENEIU   _____

14. IUHPNS   _____

15. NEGAEEVNC   _____

FUN FACT: God granted King Solomon wisdom, wealth, and honor. Solomon reigned over Israel forty years.

WORD SCRAMBLE – SHEET #37

2 CHRONICLES

The Lord protects and blesses those dedicated to Him.

1. CPERTTO   _____

2. SSBEL   _____

3. IRLDESOS   _____

4. MYAR   _____

5. LREASI   _____

6. TIORFYF   _____

7. RAGDU   _____

8. BERDOR   _____

9. ERUL   _____

10. LSOENS   _____

11. DCEDTEIA   _____

12. EFUTUR   _____

13. IMMORLA   _____

14. TIDORALY   _____

15. KNMOGDI   _____

FUN FACT: The Second Book of Chronicles has 36 chapters concerning the great revivals under kings Asa, Jehoshaphat, Joash, Hezekiah, and Josiah.

WORD SCRAMBLE – SHEET #38

ISAIAH

MEANING OF NAME: "THE LORD HAS SAVED"

1. EGSAMSE _____

2. OGD _____

3. OSEEVRNIG _____

4. OTROLCN _____

5. YRTHSIO _____

6. IOPCRNETID _____

7. JSSEU _____

8. UNETRR _____

9. PRHOETP _____

10. NSI _____

11. DIPORE _____

12. INGLSBES _____

13. IARSOV _____

14. ALIYTGMH _____

15. LODR _____

FUN FACT: Jude was a half-brother of Jesus Christ. He was a leader in the church in Jerusalem. In the Book of Jude, he writes about false teachers.

WORD SCRAMBLE – SHEET #39

MICAH

MEANING OF NAME: "WHO IS LIKE THE LORD"

In this messianic prophecy, Micah predicted the place of Christ's birth.

1. TEMLHEEHB _____

2. TLETIL _____

3. DSNUATOH _____

4. LRURE _____

5. SNATD _____

6. DEEF _____

7. KOFCL _____

8. TETRGSHN _____

9. MEASTYJ _____

10. EMNA _____

11. IBEAD _____

12. TAREG _____

13. TRHAE _____

14. CEEAP _____

15. CPYHPEOR _____

FUN FACT: James was a half-brother of Jesus. His nickname was "Just". James was a leader in the church in Jerusalem. The topic of his letter is faith.

WORD SCRAMBLE – SHEET #40

JOEL

MEANING OF NAME: "THE LORD IS GOD"

Visions shared with the people of Judah was a call to repentance.

1. COLUSTS _____

2. RMSWA _____

3. SIRPT _____

4. GNEEATIVOT _____

5. SINIOV _____

6. ROHAD _____

7. TEATAVSED _____

8. IEENNTRVE _____

9. UPHISN _____

10. PYIT _____

11. TNNIAEERGO _____

12. NLAD _____

13. PRNIEETTR _____

14. ROWRSO _____

15. LUPAEG _____

FUN FACT: The three pastoral letters are 1 Timothy, 2 Timothy and Titus.

WORD SCRAMBLE – SHEET #41

1. TREU   _____

2. LAFSE   _____

3. ILE   _____

4. NTMNUNEOEANC   _____

5. OPERW   _____

6. VPCTIEA   _____

7. BLNOE   _____

8. ATOCIONDTNRIC   _____

9. UNTERR   _____

10. LEEJMRSUA   _____

11. BYONLAB   _____

12. NOCNTROF   _____

13. YEOB   _____

14. IENSTL   _____

15. EHATD   _____

FUN FACT: The theme of Paul's letter to the Romans is righteousness.

WORD SCRAMBLE – SHEET #42

SONG OF SOLOMON

1. OELV
   _____

2. RYTOS
   _____

3. WNMAO
   _____

4. TSHRCI
   _____

5. OOAMNYGM
   _____

6. GERAMRIA
   _____

7. SFIDNRE
   _____

8. GWIENDD
   _____

9. GSNO
   _____

10. IPROSEALITHN
    _____

11. OBTREIALNCE
    _____

12. BHDNSUA
    _____

13. EIWF
    _____

14. TTMMEMNCOI
    _____

15. LEBVEEI
    _____

FUN FACT: In The Song of Solomon an overgrown garden symbolizes the sexual maturity of a young woman.

WORD SCRAMBLE – SHEET #43

PROVERBS

1. MODWSI _____

2. ADUENSNDIRTNG _____

3. UOTCNTIRNIS _____

4. OICEERNPTP _____

5. TUDEMGJN _____

6. EISTJUC _____

7. NUTAGAREE _____

8. NUIGECAD _____

9. AMRONIIFOTN _____

10. OEIISCND _____

11. NCEORNC _____

12. ONSCQEEECNU _____

13. KKWGEEONDL _____

14. LTRAMYIO _____

15. INPDEILCSI _____

FUN FACT: Matthew wrote the gospel directed to the Jews.

WORD SCRAMBLE – SHEET #44

RUTH

MEANING OF NAME: "PLEASANT"

1. OAINM   _____
2. IAKSNNM   _____
3. NNOIU   _____
4. NEINRIHCTAE   _____
5. YRMAR   _____
6. BZAO   _____
7. TESTAE   _____
8. PYELNTA   _____
9. AHTIF   _____
10. ODEB   _____
11. THEORM   _____
12. POPTSRU   _____
13. EUDATHGR   _____
14. SPNTEALA   _____
15. YBATEU   _____

FUN FACT: Ecclesiastes means "Preacher" because it contains meditations and sermons of Solomon, son of David, king of Jerusalem.

WORD SCRAMBLE – SHEET #45

SAMSON

1. NSAOSM

2. PSNOASI

3. IUOTRETPST

4. SHTNIISILPE

5. OMALR

6. LAITPSRUI

7. EKSWESAN

8. JEDUG

9. EECSRT

10. ITSGF

11. OIREPPSNOS

12. ERDIVEL

13. OTILNTPAE

14. NENCDIIT

15. SHCPYIAL

FUN FACT: John the Baptist, cousin of Jesus Christ and prophet of God, was chosen by God to herald the Messiah. He was the son of Elizabeth and Zacharias, the priest.

WORD SCRAMBLE – SHEET #46

KING DAVID'S REIGN

1. EGRMVNOENT   _____

2. YAMONRCH   _____

3. OANTNI   _____

4. RAAHNYC   _____

5. EVPOTRY   _____

6. TAHELW   _____

7. YTTORIRER   _____

8. ATLOCPIIL   _____

9. PHROSIW   _____

10. TEERNC   _____

11. ORWLD   _____

12. HBEWRE   _____

13. CAESNSTDDNE   _____

14. SCEONH   _____

15. SEJW   _____

FUN FACT: Cornelius was a Roman Centurion and the first gentile to convert to Christianity.

WORD SCRAMBLE – SHEET #47

JOSHUA
(AKA Oshea/Hoshea)
MEANING OF NAME: "WHOSE HELP IS JEHOVAH"

1. NAAACN _____

2. RISTIESLAE _____

3. PEISS _____

4. CIJHROE _____

5. JONDAR _____

6. IEVRR _____

7. ECCMIRUSIC _____

8. SSRAPEVO _____

9. CTORIVY _____

10. TNRAPPIOEAR _____

11. EHALLGNEC _____

12. ERLEDA _____

13. IPSREMO _____

14. UNESCQOT _____

15. IOVDISNI _____

FUN FACT: The word FAITH is mentioned in the bible 246 times in the NKJV. It is mentioned the most in the books of Hebrews (32) and Romans (38).

WORD SCRAMBLE – SHEET #48

DEBORAH

Deborah was the wife of Lapidoth, an Israelite from the tribe of Ephraim. She was also a prophetess and a judge. Her story is found in the book of Judges.

1. AWOMN _____
2. HPTOEESPSR _____
3. ERLEAD _____
4. EJDUG _____
5. NHTROREN _____
6. EBSRIT _____
7. ILISERATE _____
8. OTYFR _____
9. YEASR _____
10. CAPEE _____
11. ERWOP _____
12. IOITALLPC _____
13. TVEEXUCEI _____
14. LETSLVGEAII _____
15. LDIUCJAI _____

FUN FACT: King Jabin, and his commander Sisera were defeated by Israelite forces, led by Deborah's commander Barak, and a housewife named Jael.

WORD SCRAMBLE – SHEET #49

LEVITICUS

Leviticus is the third book of the Pentateuch.

1. TUNRB _____

2. ARGNI _____

3. EOSLWLPFIH _____

4. EECAP _____

5. NIS _____

6. ITCIPURNIAFO _____

7. ITGUL _____

8. OFSNSCE _____

9. OODLB _____

10. TNOEAMNTE _____

11. VRNEGIOF _____

12. RFCIESICA _____

13. GFNIOFER _____

14. NTOODEVI _____

15. SHIGTNVINKGA _____

FUN FACT: Leviticus has 27 chapters, 859 verses and 24,581 words.

WORD SCRAMBLE – SHEET #50

THE TEN COMMANDMENTS

1. OHNRO   _____
2. EMAN   _____
3. NAVI   _____
4. MDUERR   _____
5. TMREOH   _____
6. HEFART   _____
7. MITCOM   _____
8. TDLYARUE   _____
9. LTSEA   _____
10. OTCEV   _____
11. TYTEIFS   _____
12. LIOGVN   _____
13. HILAFTUF   _____
14. GODO   _____
15. OYLH   _____

Fun Fact: The Ten Commandments teach basic morality. The first four reveal what it takes to have a good relationship with God. The next six show how to have a good relationship with other people.

WORD MATCH

WORD MATCH - SHEET #1
MATCH COLUMN A WITH COLUMN B

BIBLICAL CHARACTERS

	COLUMN A			COLUMN B
1	DEBORAH	_____	A	Swallowed by Whale
2	SAMSON	_____	B	Jezebel
3	RUTH	_____	C	Delilah
4	SOLOMON	_____	D	"Call me Mara."
5	DAVID	_____	E	Upright
6	NAOMI	_____	F	Prophetess, Judge
7	ELIJAH	_____	G	Chariot of fire
8	JOB	_____	H	Defeated Goliath
9	AHAB	_____	I	Wife of Boaz
10	JONAH	_____	J	Wrote Book of Proverbs

FUN FACT: The First Book of Kings has 22 chapters and 816 verses. Chapter 8 is the longest chapter with 66 verses. Chapter 5 is the shortest chapter with 18 verses.

WORD MATCH - SHEET #2
MATCH COLUMN A WITH COLUMN B

PROPHETS/PREDICTIONS

	COLUMN A			COLUMN B
1	EZEKIEL	_____	A	Rebuilt Jerusalem's Wall; Governor
2	MICAH	_____	B	Predicted Destruction of Babylon
3	NAHUM	_____	C	Prophesied God's Judgment
4	NEHEMIAH	_____	D	Shortest book; theme: destruction of Edom
5	JEREMIAH	_____	E	The Son of God
6	ISAIAH	_____	F	Destruction of Jerusalem; restoration; Christ's birth
7	ZEPHANIAH	_____	G	Fall of Nineveh, capital of Assyrian Empire
8	JESUS	_____	H	Called the "Weeping Prophet"; Prophet to Judah
9	HABAKKUK	_____	I	Priest/Prophet; son of Buzi; dramatic visions;
10	OBADIAH	_____	J	This prophet went up to a Watchtower

FUN FACT: The four major prophets: Isaiah, Jeremiah, Ezekiel, and Daniel. The twelve minor prophets: Hosea, Joel, Amos, Obadiah, Jonah, Micah, Nahum, Habakkuk, Zephaniah, Haggai, Zechariah, and Malachi.

WORD MATCH - SHEET #3
MATCH COLUMN A WITH COLUMN B

PROPHETS

	COLUMN A			COLUMN B
1	EZRA	_____	A	Interpreted Nebuchadnezzar's dream
2	HAGGAI	_____	B	The last Old Testament book.
3	JOEL	_____	C	Saw a measuring line, woman in a basket
4	AMOS	_____	D	Speaks of rebuilding temple/glory which awaits it.
5	DANIEL	_____	E	Speaks of unfaithful wife and nation.
6	SAMUEL	_____	F	Scribe/Priest; Return of exiles; rebuilding of temple
7	ZECHARIAH	_____	G	Theme: judgment/coming of Messiah
8	JOSHUA	_____	H	Parents Hannah and Elkanah;
9	MALACHI	_____	I	Delivered Israelites to the Promised Land.
10	HOSEA	_____	J	Speaks of transgressions and judgment of nations

FUN FACT: The Old Testament book with the least number of chapters is Obadiah with one chapter consisting of 21 verses. In the book of Obadiah, the pre-exilic prophet delivered message from God to Edom.

WORD MATCH - SHEET #4
MATCH COLUMN A WITH COLUMN B

BIBLICAL CHARACTERS

	COLUMN A			COLUMN B
1	LUKE	_____	A	Apostle; Tax Collector
2	PHILIP	_____	B	Archangel
3	MARY	_____	C	Roman Governor
4	MATTHEW	_____	D	Leading Disciple
5	JOHN THE BAPTIST	_____	E	Physician; Author of Book of Acts
6	PILATE	_____	F	Was asked how to feed 5,000
7	JOSEPH	_____	G	Mother of Jesus
8	GABRIEL	_____	H	Martyr; Stoned by Mob
9	PETER	_____	I	Elizabeth's Son; Jesus' Cousin
10	STEPHEN	_____	J	Carpenter

FUN FACT: The name Malachi means "My Messenger". Malachi prophesied about John the Baptist approximately 400 years prior to his birth. (Mal 3:1)

"Behold, I send My messenger, And he will prepare the way before Me. And the Lord, whom you seek, Will suddenly come to His temple, Even the Messenger of the covenant, In whom you delight. Behold, He is coming," Says the LORD of hosts.

WORD MATCH - SHEET #5
MATCH COLUMN A WITH COLUMN B

BIBLICAL CHARACTERS

	COLUMN A			COLUMN B
1	RAHAB	_____	A	Wife of Elkanah
2	PUAH	_____	B	Sister of Aaron and Moses
3	PENINNAH	_____	C	Oldest Daughter of Laban
4	ZIPPORAH	_____	D	Harlot of Jericho
5	MILCAH	_____	E	Hebrew Midwife
6	MIRIAM	_____	F	Egyptian Maidservant of Sarah
7	LEAH	_____	G	Wife of Abraham's brother
8	HAGAR	_____	H	Moses' Ethiopian Wife
9	JAEL	_____	I	Wife of Abraham
10	SARAH	_____	J	Wife of Heber the Kenite

FUN FACT: Names for Satan; Abaddon, Apollyon, Beelzebub, Belial, The Dragon, Tempter, Deceiver, Adversary, Serpent of Old, Prince of the Power of the Air, Lucifer, Wicked One, and A Roaring Lion.

WORD MATCH - SHEET #6

MATCH COLUMN A WITH COLUMN B

BIBLICAL CHARACTERS

	COLUMN A			COLUMN B
1	BATHSHEBA	_____	A	Judge, Prophetess
2	HADASSAH	_____	B	Wife of Abraham
3	HANNAH	_____	C	Lover of Samson
4	BASEMATH	_____	D	Wife of Ananias
5	KETURAH	_____	E	Daughter of King Solomon
6	DELILAH	_____	F	Youngest Daughter of Laban
7	EVE	_____	G	Wife of Uriah the Hittite
8	SAPPHIRA	_____	H	1st Wife of Elkanah
9	DEBORAH	_____	I	First Woman God Created
10	RACHEL	_____	J	Esther

FUN FACT: The name Timothy means "Honored by God". Timothy's mother is Eunice. His grandmother is Lois. Timothy was Paul's traveling partner.

WORD MATCH - SHEET #7
MATCH COLUMN A WITH COLUMN B

BIBLICAL CHARACTERS

	COLUMN A			COLUMN B
1	AARON	_____	A	Great Hunter
2	NIMROD	_____	B	Son of Abraham/Sarah
3	ISHMAEL	_____	C	Zipporah's Father
4	ENOCH	_____	D	Giant Warriors
5	JETHRO	_____	E	Walked With God
6	METHUSALEH	_____	F	Prophet
7	ISAAC	_____	G	Moses' Brother
8	NEPHILIM	_____	H	Son of Abraham/Hagar
9	SAMUEL	_____	I	Priest
10	ZADOK	_____	J	Lived 969 Years

FUN FACT: Lazarus means "God Has Helped". Lazarus is the brother of Martha and Mary of Bethany.

WORD MATCH - SHEET #8
MATCH COLUMN A WITH COLUMN B

BIBLICAL CHARACTERS

	COLUMN A			COLUMN B
1	SOLOMON	_____	A	Persian King
2	QUEEN OF SHEBA	_____	B	16th King of Judah;
3	WIFE OF AHAB	_____	C	Prophetess
4	ELIJAH	_____	D	Chancellor to King Xerxes
5	JOSIAH	_____	E	Ate a Book
6	HAMAN	_____	F	Jeremiah's Friend
7	HULDAH	_____	G	Prophet
8	BARUCH	_____	H	Wisest Man on Earth
9	EZEKIEL	_____	I	Jezebel
10	DARIUS	_____	J	African Queen

FUN FACT: In the 13th chapter of Matthew, we find eight parables. There is the parable of the Sower, the wheat and tares, the mustard seed, the leaven, the hidden treasure, the pearl of a great price, the dragnet, and the householder.

WORD MATCH - SHEET #9
MATCH COLUMN A WITH COLUMN B

BIBLICAL CHARACTERS

	COLUMN A			COLUMN B
1	SALOME	_____	A	Brother of Mary & Martha
2	ELIZABETH	_____	B	Suffered from Mental Illness
3	JONAH	_____	C	Woman Who Ministered to Jesus
4	JAMES/JOHN	_____	D	John the Baptist's Father
5	NICODEMUS	_____	E	Wife of Zebedee
6	SUSANNA	_____	F	Fishermen
7	ZACCHAEUS	_____	G	Zechariah's Wife
8	ZECHARIAH	_____	H	Swallowed By a Whale
9	MARY MAGDALENE	_____	I	Pharisee leader in Bethlehem
10	LAZARUS	_____	J	Climbed Tree to See Jesus

FUN FACT: The name Zechariah means "The Lord Remembers". The book of Zechariah has fourteen chapters consisting of 210 verses.

WORD MATCH - SHEET #10
MATCH COLUMN A WITH COLUMN B

BIBLICAL CHARACTERS

	COLUMN A			COLUMN B
1	CLEOPHAS	_____	A	Anointed By Elijah
2	CORNELIUS	_____	B	Husband of Naomi
3	ELHANAN	_____	C	Name for the Messiah
4	ELISHA	_____	D	Son of Zerubbabel
5	ELIMELECH	_____	E	Son of Lamech & Adah
6	EMMANUEL	_____	F	Roman Centurion
7	HANANIAH	_____	G	Ruler of Synagogue
8	JABAL	_____	H	Warrior; Slew Goliath's Brother
9	JAIRUS	_____	I	Husband of Mary's Sister
10	KEZIA	_____	J	2nd Daughter of Job

FUN FACT: In the book of Proverbs, Jesus is portrayed as our Wisdom.

WORD MATCH - SHEET #11
MATCH COLUMN A WITH COLUMN B

BIBLICAL CHARACTERS

	COLUMN A			COLUMN B
1	PETER	_____	A	Greek; Converted by Paul
2	THOMAS	_____	B	Aquilla's Wife; Tentmaker
3	GERSHOM	_____	C	Paul's Traveling Companion
4	PRISCILLA	_____	D	King of Judea and Samaria
5	SCEVA	_____	E	Called "The Rock"
6	JESUS	_____	F	Roman Goddess
7	AGRIPPA	_____	G	Doubtful Disciple
8	SILAS	_____	H	Son of God
9	DIANA	_____	I	Priest With Seven Sons
10	TITUS	_____	J	Son of Moses

FUN FACT: Apostle Paul wrote The Book of Romans, 1 Corinthians, 2 Corinthians, Galatians, Ephesians, Philippians, Colossians, 1 Thessalonians, 2 Thessalonians, 1 Timothy, 2 Timothy, Titus, and Philemon.

WORD MATCH - SHEET #12
MATCH COLUMN A WITH COLUMN B

BIBLICAL CHARACTERS

	COLUMN A			COLUMN B
1	ISSACHAR	_____	A	Brother of Jesus and James
2	LYDIA	_____	B	Brother of Christ; called the Just
3	QUIRINUS	_____	C	Superior to Angels
4	RIZPAH	_____	D	Descendant of Dan
5	JUDE	_____	E	King of Jerusalem; Priest
6	JAMES	_____	F	One who Speaks or Interprets
7	JESUS	_____	G	Roman Governor of Syria
8	MELCHIZEDEK	_____	H	Woman of Thyatira
9	PROPHET	_____	I	King Saul's Concubine
10	DANITES	_____	J	5TH Son of Jacob

FUN FACT: The word "and" is listed 1,375 times in the book of Mark.

WORD MATCH - SHEET #13
MATCH COLUMN A WITH COLUMN B

BIBLICAL CHARACTERS

	COLUMN A			COLUMN B
1	JOCHEBED	_____	A	Son & Successor of Amon
2	JOKSHAN	_____	B	Eleventh Son of Jacob
3	JONATHAN	_____	C	Leader of the Israelites
4	JOSIAH	_____	D	Wife of Esau
5	JOTHAM	_____	E	Fourth Son of Jacob & Leah
6	JOSHUA	_____	F	Son of Saul
7	JUBAL	_____	G	Son of Abraham & Keturah
8	MAHALATH	_____	H	Youngest Son of Gideon
9	JOSEPH	_____	I	Son of Lamech
10	JUDAH	_____	J	Mother of Moses

FUN FACT: The word "kingdom" is listed 55 times in the Gospel of Matthew.

WORD MATCH - SHEET #14
MATCH COLUMN A WITH COLUMN B

BIBLICAL CHARACTERS

COLUMN A		COLUMN B
1 JOHN THE BAPTIST	_____	A One of the Sons of Cush
2 JOHN THE APOSTLE	_____	B Seaport of Pamphilia
3 NATHANAEL	_____	C Octavius, Emperor of Rome
4 SEBA	_____	D Queen of Ethiopia
5 ATTALIA	_____	E Sold Birthright to Brother
6 AUGUSTUS	_____	F Followers of Christ
7 CANDACE	_____	G A City of Greece
8 CHRISTIANS	_____	H Confessed Christ's Messiahship
9 CORINTH	_____	I Son of Zacharias & Elizabeth
10 ESAU	_____	J Son of Zebedee & Salome

FUN FACT: While delivering his Sermon on the Mount Jesus stated "I say unto you" fourteen times.

WORD MATCH - SHEET #15
MATCH COLUMN A WITH COLUMN B

BIBLICAL CHARACTERS

	COLUMN A			COLUMN B
1	TUBAL-CAIN	_____	A	First Judge of Israel
2	JABEL	_____	B	God's covenant fulfilled through him
3	JUBAL	_____	C	Abraham's Father
4	OTHNIEL	_____	D	Father of tent dwellers/Herdsmen
5	JABIN	_____	E	Judge; Led Israelites from oppression
6	GIDEON	_____	F	Father of craftsmen in bronze/iron
7	ISHMAEL	_____	G	Abraham's first son
8	ISAAC	_____	H	King of Canaan
9	TERAH	_____	I	Father of musicians
10	SAMSON	_____	J	Farmer/Judge

FUN FACT: The word church comes from the word "ecclesia" which means "called out ones".

WORD MATCH SHEET #16
MATCH COLUMN A WITH COLUMN B

MOTHER AND CHILD

	COLUMN A			COLUMN B
1	TAMAR	_____	A	John the Baptist
2	RACHEL	_____	B	Ishmael
3	REBEKEH	_____	C	Zerah (AKA Zarah)
4	SALOME	_____	D	James/John
5	MARY	_____	E	Chileab
6	ABIGAIL	_____	F	Benjamin
7	HANNAH	_____	G	Obed
8	HAGAR	_____	H	Samuel
9	ELIZABETH	_____	I	Esau/Jacob
10	RUTH	_____	J	Jesus

FUN FACT: Jesus used seven I AM statements in the book of John. These statements proved His deity. Our sovereign Savior said the following:

- I AM the bread of life (John 6:35)
- I AM the light of the world (John 8:12)
- I AM the gate (John 10:7)
- I AM the good shepherd (John 10:11, 14)
- I AM the resurrection, and the life (John 11:25)
- I AM the way, the truth, and the life (John 14:6)
- I AM the true vine (John 15:1)

WORD MATCH SHEET #17
MATCH COLUMN A WITH COLUMN B

FATHER AND SON

	COLUMN A			COLUMN B
1	METHUSELAH	_____	A	David
2	MANOAH	_____	B	Jacob/Esau
3	JESSE	_____	C	Manasseh
4	DAVID	_____	D	Asa
5	JUDAH	_____	E	Lamech
6	ISAAC	_____	F	Abijah
7	JOSEPH	_____	G	Solomon
8	SOLOMON	_____	H	Perez/Zerah
9	REHOBOAM	_____	I	Samson
10	ABIJAH	_____	J	Rehoboam

FUN FACT: Ezekiel's parable about dry bones symbolized the spiritual renewal of Israel.

WORD MATCH SHEET #18
MATCH COLUMN A WITH COLUMN B

HUSBAND AND WIFE

	COLUMN A			COLUMN B
1	LAMECH	_____	A	Naomi
2	JOSEPH	_____	B	Milcah
3	HEBER	_____	C	Ruth
4	HOSEA	_____	D	Jael
5	MAHLON	_____	E	Jochebed
6	ELIMELECH	_____	F	Judith
7	AMRAM	_____	G	Asenath
8	NAHOR	_____	H	Naamah
9	SOLOMON	_____	I	Zillah
10	MANASSEH	_____	J	Gomer

FUN FACT: Ezekiel's parable about the shipwreck foretold the judgment of Tyre.

WORD MATCH - SHEET #19
MATCH COLUMN A WITH COLUMN B

WHOSE VISION/DREAM?

	COLUMN A			COLUMN B
1	CHIEF BAKER	_____	A	3 baskets; baked goods
2	PETER	_____	B	Sheaves bowing
3	EZEKIEL	_____	C	Tree in the midst of the earth
4	CHIEF BUTLER	_____	D	Sheet descend full of animals
5	NEBUCHADNEZZAR	_____	E	7 ugly cows devour 7 fine cows
6	JOSEPH	_____	F	Sight restored by Ananias
7	JOEL	_____	G	Vine with 3 branches, ripe grapes
8	PHAROAH	_____	H	The Coming Day of the Lord
9	AMOS	_____	I	Five visions of doom
10	SAUL	_____	J	25 men worshipping the sun

FUN FACT: Ezekiel's parable about the two harlots symbolized the spiritual adultery of Israel and Judah.

WORD MATCH - SHEET #20
MATCH COLUMN A WITH COLUMN B

WHOSE VISION/DREAM?

	COLUMN A			COLUMN B
1	AMOS	_____	A	Angels ascending/descending
2	ZECHARIAH	_____	B	Holy Jerusalem
3	JESUS	_____	C	Burning Bush
4	JOHN	_____	D	Angel of the Lord in a dream
5	MOSES	_____	E	Basket of Summer Fruit
6	JACOB	_____	F	Chariot of fire
7	ELIJAH/ELISHA	_____	G	Fire come from heaven
8	JOSEPH	_____	H	Spirit of God descending
9	ELIJAH	_____	I	Angel of the Lord ascending
10	MANOAH/WIFE	_____	J	Four Horns

FUN FACT: Abimelech means "My Father is King" Abimelech is the son of Gideon by a concubine. He had 70 half-brothers. He murdered his half-brothers and was later killed after a woman dropped a millstone on his head.

WORD MATCH - SHEET #21
MATCH COLUMN A WITH COLUMN B

KINGS - DAVID AND SOLOMON

	COLUMN A			COLUMN B
1	GAD	_____	A	Son of Solomon; reigned in Judah
2	JOAB	_____	B	King following his David's death
3	JOASH	_____	C	Solomon's adversary;
4	HIRAM	_____	D	King David's son by Haggith
5	REHOBOAM	_____	E	King of Jerusalem
6	REZON	_____	F	King David's Seer;
7	ADONIJAH	_____	G	Owned threshing floor
8	HADAD	_____	H	Reigned over Syria;
9	KING SOLOMON	_____	I	Phoenician King of Tyre
10	ARAUNAH	_____	J	Commander of King David's army

FUN FACT: Jephthah means "He Will Open". He was the son of a harlot. He made a vow to the Lord that resulted in the loss of his daughter.

WORD MATCH - SHEET #22
MATCH COLUMN A WITH COLUMN B

	COLUMN A			COLUMN B
1	JOSEPH	_____	A	Son of Solomon;
2	ISHMAEL	_____	B	Prophet
3	ABIMELECH	_____	C	Archer
4	REHOBOAM	_____	D	Herdsman
5	CAIN	_____	E	Priest
6	NATHAN	_____	F	Carpenter
7	ABEL	_____	G	King of the Philistines
8	JEHOIADA	_____	H	Farmer
9	PHICOL	_____	I	King of Israel
10	JOASH	_____	J	Cmdr. of Abimelech's Army

FUN FACT: Samson means "Sunny". Samson was the 14th judge of Israel. Samson judged Israel for twenty years.

WORD MATCH - SHEET #23
MATCH COLUMN A WITH COLUMN B

KNOWN BY ANOTHER NAME

	COLUMN A			COLUMN B
1	JACOB	_____	A	Zaphnath-Paaneah
2	SAUL	_____	B	Abraham
3	BELTESHAZZAR	_____	C	Jerubbaal
4	SIMON (Cephas)	_____	D	Hananiah
5	JOSEPH	_____	E	Sarah
6	ABRAM	_____	F	Azariah
7	GIDEON	_____	G	Peter
8	SARAI	_____	H	Daniel
9	SHADRACH	_____	I	Paul
10	ABED-NEGO	_____	J	Israel

FUN FACT: Phinehas means "The Nubian". Phinehas was the son of Eleazar; grandson of Aaron and Elisheba. Phinehas was a priest. He became the third high priest of Israel and served 19 years.

WORD MATCH SHEET #24
MATCH COLUMN A WITH COLUMN B

TEN PLAGUES OF EGYPT

	COLUMN A			COLUMN B
1	1st Plague of Egypt	_____	A	Flies Swarming the Houses
2	2nd Plague of Egypt	_____	B	Death of Firstborn
3	3rd Plague of Egypt	_____	C	Water Turning to Blood
4	4th Plague of Egypt	_____	D	Lice Tormenting People/Animals
5	5th Plague of Egypt	_____	E	Boils Breaking on the Egyptians
6	6th Plague of Egypt	_____	F	Frogs Infesting the Land
7	7th Plague of Egypt	_____	G	Darkness Covering Land Three Days
8	8th Plague of Egypt	_____	H	Livestock Pestilence, Killing Cattle
9	9th Plague of Egypt	_____	I	Locusts Devouring Vegetation
10	10th Plague of Egypt	_____	J	Hail Destroying Crops

FUN FACT: Korah means "Baldness". Korah was a descendent of Kohath of the tribe of Levi. He was also the first cousin of Moses.

WORD MATCH SHEET #25
MATCH COLUMN A WITH COLUMN B

DAVID'S KIN

COLUMN A		COLUMN B	
1	ABIGAIL (1) _____	A	8th Wife; Mother of King Solomon
2	MAACAH _____	B	Daughter; Mother Maacah;
3	ABIHAIL _____	C	3rd Wife; Mother of Amnon
4	ABITAL _____	D	7th Wife; Mother of 6th son Ithream
5	AHINOAM _____	E	2nd Wife; Mother of son Chileab
6	BATHSHEBA _____	F	5th Wife; Mother of son Adonijah
7	EGLAH _____	G	Daughter-in-law; Married Jerimoth
8	HAGGITH _____	H	1st Wife; Daughter of King Saul
9	MICHAL _____	I	4th Wife; Mother of Absalom
10	TAMAR _____	J	6th Wife; Mother of son Shephatiah

FUN FACT: Miriam means "Stubbornness" or "Rebellion". Miriam was the daughter of Amram and Jochebed. She was the older sister of Moses and Aaron.

WORD MATCH SHEET #26
MATCH COLUMN A WITH COLUMN B

TITLES FOR GOD – FOUND IN THE OLD TESTAMENT

	COLUMN A		COLUMN B
1	JEHOVAH ELOHIM	_____	A Mighty God
2	JEHOVAH JIREH	_____	B The Lord our healer.
3	JEHOVAH NISSI	_____	C The Lord of hosts.
4	JEHOVAH ROPHEKA	_____	D God Almighty
5	JEHOVAH SHALOM	_____	E The Lord will provide.
6	JEHOVAH SABAOTH	_____	F The Lord our peace.
7	JEHOVAH SHAMMAH	_____	G The Lord Most High.
8	JEHOVAH ELYON	_____	H The Eternal One or Creator.
9	EL SHADDAI	_____	I The Lord our banner.
10	El GIBHOR	_____	J The Lord is present.

FUN FACT: Benjamin means "Son of the Right Hand" or "Son of the South". Benjamin is the son of Rachel and Jacob. His mother died during childbirth.

WORD MATCH SHEET #27
MATCH COLUMN A WITH COLUMN B

TITLES FOR GOD – FOUND IN THE OLD TESTAMENT

COLUMN A		COLUMN B
1 JEHOVAH ROHI	_____	A The Lord our Sovereign;
2 JEHOVAH ELOHEENU	_____	B The Lord our Sanctifier.
3 JEHOVAH TSIDKENU	_____	C The Lord my God.
4 JEHOVAH MEKADDISHKEM	_____	D God Who Sees Me
5 JEHOVAH HOSEENU	_____	E Everlasting God
6 JEHOVAH ELOHAY	_____	F The Lord my Shepherd.
7 JEHOVAH ELOHEKA	_____	G The Lord our Righteousness
8 ADONAI-JEHOVAH	_____	H The Lord our God.
9 EL ROI	_____	I The Lord thy God.
10 EL OLAM	_____	J The Lord our Maker.

FUN FACT: Methuselah means "Man of the Javelin". Methuselah was the son of Enoch. He was an ancestor of Noah and Jesus Christ. He is the oldest man mentioned in the bible having lived for 969 years.

WORD SEARCH

WORD SEARCH – SHEET #1

OLD TESTAMENT

The Old Testament begins with the creation of earth and the first humans, Adam and Eve. The couple were banished from the Garden of Eden because of sin.

AARON
ABRAHAM
ADAM
ARK
BOOK OF GENESIS
COVENANT
DESCENDANTS
DISOBEDIENCE
ESAU
EVE
EXILE
GARDEN OF EDEN
GREAT FLOOD
ISAAC
ISHMAEL
JACOB
JEWISH
KINGDOM
MIDIAN
MOSES
MOUNT SINAI
PASSOVER
REBEKAH
SABBATH
SARAH
SERPENT
TREE OF
KNOWLEDGE
TREE OF LIFE
TOWER OF BABEL

B	O	O	K	O	F	G	E	N	E	S	I	S	A	B
M	O	U	N	T	S	I	N	A	I	C	D	U	E	F
H	G	A	R	D	E	N	O	F	E	D	E	N	S	D
I	J	M	A	X	S	O	W	E	R	I	H	D	M	V
A	B	R	A	H	A	M	T	U	X	S	Q	A	R	K
R	L	O	J	E	W	I	S	H	P	O	D	Y	U	O
K	I	N	G	D	O	M	A	M	F	B	R	N	H	I
W	V	Q	U	E	N	C	C	O	V	E	N	A	N	T
S	A	B	B	A	T	H	F	S	G	D	J	W	I	L
E	X	M	L	B	A	R	T	E	K	I	S	A	A	C
R	T	U	C	E	B	P	O	S	T	E	Y	F	p	K
P	R	J	M	L	L	S	V	R	I	N	U	K	A	Z
E	S	A	U	B	E	X	I	L	E	C	M	I	S	A
N	F	C	G	H	T	I	J	U	O	E	I	S	S	N
T	G	O	N	W	L	A	D	A	M	R	D	H	O	T
O	S	B	P	S	C	N	Y	I	Q	K	I	M	V	R
D	A	A	R	O	N	S	R	L	E	A	A	A	E	E
G	R	E	A	T	F	L	O	O	D	P	N	E	R	E
E	A	V	H	A	S	O	A	H	D	M	R	L	T	O
F	H	R	E	B	E	K	A	H	E	F	Y	S	L	F
I	K	J	T	O	W	E	R	O	F	B	A	B	E	L
D	E	S	C	E	N	D	A	N	T	S	E	O	T	I
R	A	C	H	E	L	C	H	U	R	N	V	P	N	F
T	R	E	E	O	F	K	N	O	W	L	E	D	G	E

WORD SEARCH – SHEET #2

TWELVE TRIBES AND TWELVE PRINCES

REUBEN
SIMEON
LEVI (Not Numbered)
JUDAH
DAN
NAPHTALI
GAD
ASHER
ISSACHAR
ZEBULUN
JOSEPH (Not Numbered)
BENJAMIN
JACOB (Patriarch)
MANASSEH
EPHRAIM
ELIZUR
SHELUMIEL
NAHSHON
NETHANEEL
ELIAB
ELISHAMA
GAMALIEL
ABIDAN
AHIEZER
ELIASAPH
AHIRA
PAGIEL
TRIBES
PRINCES
TWELVE

Z	E	B	U	L	U	N	J	O	K	M	L	E	V	I
A	L	E	N	M	D	A	N	P	F	Q	G	R	W	S
H	I	N	D	A	L	P	Y	B	C	R	A	D	I	S
I	Z	J	E	R	V	H	D	U	J	U	D	A	H	A
E	U	A	R	T	X	T	I	M	Y	F	S	G	O	C
Z	R	M	O	H	W	A	J	R	E	U	B	E	N	H
E	X	I	N	A	O	L	H	D	L	E	L	I	S	A
R	L	N	E	U	S	I	M	E	O	N	O	J	W	R
U	M	B	R	G	A	Q	R	P	T	A	V	N	O	T
P	A	G	I	E	L	G	D	H	I	L	E	A	X	P
Z	E	B	R	A	J	H	S	R	P	K	R	H	U	C
J	O	S	E	P	H	U	M	A	N	A	S	S	E	H
S	H	A	R	K	I	T	S	I	W	S	Y	H	L	R
P	R	I	N	C	E	S	O	M	G	H	K	O	I	U
N	E	C	T	A	R	I	N	E	K	E	L	N	A	W
G	A	M	A	L	I	E	L	T	U	R	N	O	B	X
N	I	C	K	P	O	L	Y	C	A	L	E	B	P	U
S	H	E	L	U	M	I	E	L	N	P	Q	R	S	G
T	R	A	N	S	F	A	P	O	P	U	L	J	R	P
I	A	V	U	I	A	B	I	D	A	N	T	A	A	S
C	T	P	M	T	R	I	B	E	S	H	D	C	I	T
E	Q	N	O	E	L	I	A	S	A	P	H	O	N	W
F	R	A	N	K	E	N	C	E	N	S	E	B	F	E
E	L	I	S	H	A	M	A	M	E	L	T	C	A	L
M	Y	R	W	Q	L	S	T	A	H	I	R	A	L	V
N	E	T	H	A	N	E	E	L	P	E	O	D	L	E

WORD SEARCH – SHEET #3

SACRIFICES AND OFFERINGS

ALTAR
AROMA
ATONEMENT
BLOOD
BUILT
BURNT
CHRIST
COMMITMENT
CONFESS
DEVOTION
FELLOWSHIP
FORGIVEN
GOD
GRAIN
GUILT
ISRAELITES
LIVESTOCK
OFFERINGS
PEACE
PIGEONS
PRIEST
PURIFICATION
SACRIFICES
SIN
SYMBOLIZES
TABERNACLE
TURTLEDOVES
UNCLEANNESS
VIOLATION

S	A	C	R	I	F	I	C	E	S	M	L	E	V	O
Y	T	L	N	M	O	A	N	P	I	Q	G	R	W	F
M	O	I	P	A	R	P	Y	B	N	R	N	D	I	F
B	N	V	R	R	G	H	D	U	J	O	D	A	H	E
O	E	E	I	T	I	T	I	M	I	E	S	L	O	R
L	M	S	E	H	V	A	J	T	G	B	F	T	L	I
I	E	T	S	A	E	L	A	N	I	O	A	A	S	N
Z	N	O	T	U	N	C	M	E	O	N	D	R	W	G
E	T	C	R	G	I	O	R	P	T	A	V	N	O	S
S	A	K	I	F	L	N	D	H	A	R	O	M	A	P
Z	E	B	I	A	J	F	S	R	P	B	U	R	N	T
J	G	R	E	P	H	E	M	A	T	A	B	W	S	H
S	U	A	R	K	I	S	S	N	W	S	Y	I	L	G
P	I	X	N	C	E	S	E	M	G	X	R	N	I	R
B	L	O	O	D	R	M	N	E	K	H	L	M	A	A
G	T	M	A	L	T	E	L	T	C	R	N	O	B	I
N	I	C	K	I	O	V	I	O	L	A	T	I	O	N
S	H	E	M	U	P	I	G	E	O	N	S	Y	C	G
T	R	M	N	I	S	R	A	E	L	I	T	E	S	D
I	O	V	U	T	U	R	T	L	E	D	O	V	E	S
C	T	P	M	G	R	I	K	E	S	P	E	A	C	E
L	E	G	I	O	I	V	I	C	T	O	R	Y	N	B
D	E	V	O	T	I	O	N	E	N	S	E	R	F	U
U	N	C	L	E	A	N	N	E	S	S	T	C	A	I
T	A	B	E	R	N	A	C	L	E	I	R	A	L	L
F	E	L	L	O	W	S	H	I	P	E	O	D	X	T

WORD SEARCH – SHEET #4

1 SAMUEL

ADVERSARY		E	L	K	A	N	A	H	J	O	K	M	H	A	I	R
AFFLICTION		R	A	M	A	H	D	A	N	P	V	Q	G	R	W	S
ANOINTED		H	I	N	D	A	L	P	E	N	I	N	N	A	H	D
BEERSHEBA		H	A	N	N	A	H	H	X	U	S	U	D	A	H	S
CHERUBIM		M	U	A	R	T	X	T	A	M	I	E	S	W	O	A
EXALT		A	R	M	O	H	W	A	L	A	O	B	F	O	L	M
ELKANAH		I	X	I	N	A	O	L	T	D	N	E	L	R	S	U
GRIEF		D	L	A	F	F	L	I	C	T	I	O	N	S	W	E
HAIR		S	H	I	L	O	H	Q	U	P	T	A	V	H	O	L
HANNAH		E	A	G	I	E	O	G	D	H	I	L	E	I	X	P
HOPNI		R	E	B	R	A	P	H	S	R	P	K	B	P	U	W
KING		V	O	S	E	P	N	U	H	A	N	A	E	P	E	I
MAIDSERVANT		A	H	A	R	K	I	C	S	I	W	S	X	E	L	C
PENINNAH		N	R	I	N	C	E	K	I	N	G	H	O	D	I	K
PHILISTINES		T	E	C	T	A	R	I	N	E	K	E	I	M	A	E
PHINEHAS		G	A	M	C	H	E	R	U	B	I	M	C	O	B	D
PROPHET		B	E	E	R	S	H	E	B	A	A	L	E	B	P	U
RAMAH		S	H	E	L	U	M	I	E	L	N	P	Q	R	S	G
RAZOR		T	R	A	N	S	R	A	Z	O	R	U	L	A	R	A
SAMUEL		I	A	V	U	G	R	I	E	F	A	N	T	U	A	N
SACRIFICE		S	A	C	R	I	F	I	C	E	S	Y	D	F	I	O
SHILOH		E	Q	N	O	E	L	P	H	I	N	E	H	A	S	I
VINEYARD		P	R	O	P	H	E	T	C	E	N	S	E	R	F	N
VISION		K	U	J	S	H	A	V	I	N	E	Y	A	R	D	T
WICKED		P	H	I	L	I	S	T	I	N	E	S	R	A	L	E
WORSHIPPED		A	D	V	E	R	S	A	R	Y	P	E	O	D	U	D

2 SAMUEL

ABISHAI
ABSALOM
AHIMAAZ
AHITHOPHEL
BATTLE
CAPTAINS
CHARIOTS
CONCUBINES
CONSPIRACY
COUNSELOR
GILONITE
JERUSALEM
JOAB
JONATHAN
KING DAVID
KINGDOM
MEPHIBOSHETH
RAISINS
SERVANT
SAUL
TAMAR
TEREBINTH
WEEPING
WINE
ZERUIAH
ZIBA

A	B	S	A	L	O	M	J	O	K	M	J	O	A	B
A	L	E	N	M	D	A	N	P	I	Q	E	R	B	S
H	I	N	D	A	L	P	Y	B	N	R	R	D	I	Z
C	A	P	T	A	I	N	S	U	G	U	U	A	S	E
E	H	A	R	T	X	T	I	M	D	E	S	G	H	R
Z	I	M	K	H	W	A	J	A	A	B	A	E	A	U
E	M	I	I	A	O	L	H	D	V	E	L	I	I	I
R	A	N	N	U	S	I	M	E	I	N	E	J	W	A
U	A	B	G	G	A	Q	R	P	D	A	M	N	O	H
P	Z	G	D	E	L	G	D	H	I	L	E	A	X	P
Z	E	B	O	A	J	G	I	L	O	N	I	T	E	C
J	O	S	M	P	H	U	M	A	N	A	S	S	E	O
M	E	P	H	I	B	O	S	H	E	T	H	O	L	U
J	O	N	A	T	H	A	N	M	G	H	K	N	I	N
T	E	R	E	B	I	N	T	H	K	E	L	M	A	S
G	A	M	A	L	R	A	I	S	I	N	S	O	B	E
N	I	C	K	P	O	L	Y	C	A	L	E	B	P	L
S	H	E	L	U	M	I	E	L	N	P	Q	R	S	O
C	O	N	C	U	B	I	N	E	S	U	L	A	R	R
I	A	V	U	I	A	B	A	T	T	L	E	T	A	S
C	T	P	M	T	R	I	B	S	E	R	V	A	N	T
S	A	U	L	E	L	I	W	I	N	E	H	M	N	W
F	R	A	W	E	E	P	I	N	G	S	E	A	F	Z
C	O	N	S	P	I	R	A	C	Y	L	T	R	A	I
M	Y	R	W	C	H	A	R	I	O	T	S	A	L	B
A	H	I	T	H	O	P	H	E	L	E	O	D	L	A

WORD SEARCH – SHEET #6

THE BOOK OF PSALMS

The Book of Psalms contains 42,713 words, 2,461 verses and 150 chapters.

ANOINT
ASSEMBLY
CONGREGATION
DECEITFULLY
EARTH
EVERLASTING
GENERATION
HABITATION
HEART
KING OF GLORY
LIGHT
MERCY
MUSICIAN
PASTURES
POTSHERD
REDEEM
RIGHTEOUSNESS
SACRIFICE
SALVATION
SHADOW
SHEPHERD
STRENGTH
VALLEY
VINDICATE
WAR
WORSHIP

M	U	S	I	C	I	A	N	O	K	M	L	E	D	S
E	L	T	N	M	D	N	N	P	F	Q	G	R	E	A
R	I	R	D	R	L	O	Y	O	C	R	A	I	C	L
C	Z	E	E	E	V	I	D	T	J	U	D	G	E	V
Y	U	N	R	D	I	N	I	S	Y	E	S	H	I	A
Z	R	G	O	E	N	T	J	H	E	A	R	T	T	T
A	X	T	N	E	D	L	H	E	L	E	L	E	F	I
S	L	H	E	M	I	I	M	R	O	N	O	O	U	O
S	M	B	R	G	C	Q	R	D	T	A	V	U	L	N
E	V	E	R	L	A	S	T	I	N	G	E	S	L	P
M	E	B	R	A	T	H	D	R	P	K	R	N	Y	K
B	O	S	E	P	E	R	M	A	N	C	S	E	E	I
L	H	G	E	N	E	R	A	T	I	O	N	S	L	N
Y	R	I	N	H	E	S	O	M	G	N	K	S	I	G
N	E	C	P	A	R	I	N	E	K	G	H	M	A	O
G	A	E	A	L	I	G	H	T	U	R	A	O	B	F
N	H	C	S	P	O	L	Y	C	A	E	B	B	P	G
S	H	E	T	U	M	I	E	E	N	G	I	R	S	L
T	R	A	U	S	F	A	C	O	P	A	T	A	R	O
I	A	V	R	I	A	I	I	W	A	T	A	W	A	R
C	T	P	E	T	F	I	B	O	E	I	T	F	I	Y
E	Q	N	S	I	L	I	A	R	A	O	I	K	N	W
F	R	A	R	K	E	N	C	S	R	N	O	R	F	E
E	L	C	S	H	A	M	A	H	T	L	N	C	A	L
M	A	R	W	Q	L	S	T	I	H	I	R	A	L	V
S	H	A	D	O	W	E	E	P	V	A	L	L	E	Y

WORD SEARCH – SHEET #7

GENESIS - REVELATION

There are 66 books in the bible (39 Old Testament and 27 New Testament).
There are 1,189 chapters in the bible (929 Old Testament and 260 New Testament).

COMMANDMENTS	D	O	M	I	N	I	O	N	O	K	M	L	E	V	P
CREATION	E	L	J	E	R	I	C	H	O	F	Q	G	R	W	A
DAY OF ATONEMENT	I	I	R	F	E	L	L	O	W	S	H	I	P	I	T
DEITY	T	Z	A	E	R	V	H	G	U	J	U	D	A	H	R
DOMINION	Y	U	N	L	E	A	V	E	N	E	D	S	G	O	I
EGYPTIANS	Z	I	G	G	U	R	A	T	A	G	B	F	E	S	A
EXODUS	L	X	I	N	A	O	L	H	D	L	E	L	T	S	R
FELLOWSHIP	C	L	P	R	E	A	C	H	E	D	N	N	J	W	C
GENEALOGY	R	M	B	R	G	A	Q	R	P	T	E	V	D	O	H
GIDEON	E	A	G	I	D	E	O	N	H	M	L	E	A	X	A
GLORY	A	E	B	R	A	J	H	S	D	P	K	R	Y	U	L
JERICHO	T	E	S	T	A	M	E	N	T	N	A	S	O	E	Z
JESUS	I	H	A	R	K	I	A	S	I	W	S	H	F	L	E
JUDAH	O	R	I	N	C	M	S	G	L	O	R	Y	A	I	G
PATRIARCHAL	N	E	C	T	M	R	I	N	E	R	E	L	T	A	Y
PENTECOST	N	A	M	O	L	J	E	L	T	S	R	N	O	B	P
PREACHED	G	I	C	K	P	E	L	Y	C	H	L	E	N	P	T
RAHAB	E	H	E	L	U	S	I	E	L	I	P	R	E	S	I
REMNANT	N	R	A	N	S	U	A	P	O	P	U	A	M	T	A
RENEW	E	X	O	D	U	S	B	I	D	A	N	H	E	R	N
SPIRITUALLY	A	T	P	M	T	R	E	N	E	W	H	A	N	U	S
TESTAMENT	L	Q	N	O	E	L	I	A	S	A	P	B	T	M	W
TRUMPETS	O	R	P	E	N	T	E	C	O	S	T	E	R	P	E
UNLEAVENED	G	L	I	S	H	A	M	A	M	E	L	T	C	E	L
WORSHIP	Y	Y	R	E	M	N	A	N	T	H	I	R	A	T	V
ZIGGURAT	N	S	P	I	R	I	T	U	A	L	L	Y	D	S	E

WORD SEARCH – SHEET #8

THE NUMBER TWELVE – GOVERNMENTAL PERFECTION

The number twelve is used one hundred eighty-seven times in the bible. Genesis (8), Exodus (7), Leviticus (1), Numbers (17), Deuteronomy (1), Joshua (11), Judges (2), 2 Samuel (4), 1 Kings (10), 2 Kings (2), 1 Chronicles (26), 2 Chronicles (7), Ezra (6), Nehemiah (2), Esther (1), Psalms (1), Jeremiah (2), Ezekiel (3), Daniel (1), Matthew (13), Mark (14), Luke (13), John (6), Acts (5), 1 Corinthians (1), James (1) and Revelation (22). One Old Testament book has 12 chapters. Do you know which book that is? Hint: Book tells a story of a young man in a lion's den.

ADBON
APOSTLES
BULLS
CAKES
CHURCHES
DEBORAH
DISCIPLES
EHUD
ELON
FOUNDATIONS
FRUITS
GATES
GIDEON
GOVERNORS
HEMORRHAGE
IZBAN
JAIR
JEPHTHAH
LAMPSTANDS
LEGION OF ANGELS
MINOR PROPHETS
MONTHS
OTHNIEL
OXEN
PRINCES
RAMS
SAMSON
SCROLLS
SHAMGAR
SIGNS

SPIES
STARS
STONES
TOLA

TRIBES
YEARS

O	T	H	N	I	E	L	J	G	A	T	E	S	V	I
A	L	E	N	M	H	R	A	M	S	J	G	R	W	Z
H	I	N	D	A	U	P	Y	B	C	R	S	D	I	B
I	J	J	E	R	D	E	B	O	R	A	H	A	H	A
E	A	Y	R	T	X	L	I	M	Y	E	A	R	S	N
G	I	D	E	O	N	A	S	A	G	B	M	E	L	H
E	R	I	N	A	O	M	O	D	M	E	G	I	M	W
J	L	N	E	U	S	P	N	T	O	L	A	J	I	E
E	L	O	N	G	A	S	S	P	N	A	R	N	N	L
P	A	G	I	E	M	T	D	H	T	L	E	J	O	L
H	B	O	W	L	S	A	W	R	H	K	H	L	R	S
T	O	S	E	P	O	N	M	T	S	A	E	E	P	H
H	H	A	R	K	N	D	S	R	W	S	M	G	R	F
A	D	B	O	N	E	S	O	I	G	I	O	I	O	O
H	E	C	T	A	R	I	N	B	K	G	R	O	P	U
C	H	U	R	C	H	E	S	E	U	R	N	H	N
D	I	S	C	I	P	L	E	S	A	S	H	O	E	D
S	H	E	L	U	M	I	E	L	O	P	A	F	T	A
A	P	O	S	T	L	E	S	O	X	U	G	A	S	T
I	A	V	T	I	A	B	P	D	E	N	E	N	A	I
C	T	P	O	T	R	K	I	E	N	H	D	G	I	O
E	Q	N	N	E	L	L	E	S	A	P	H	E	N	N
C	A	K	E	S	E	P	S	C	R	O	L	L	S	S
E	L	I	S	G	O	V	E	R	N	O	R	S	A	L
B	U	L	L	S	L	S	T	A	R	S	R	A	L	V
P	R	I	N	C	E	S	E	L	F	R	U	I	T	S

WORD SEARCH – SHEET #9

BABYLON
CHRIST
DIVISION
FAITH
FATHER
GRACE
GOODNESS
HARVEST
IDOLATRY
INIQUITY
JUDGMENT
LORD
MESSIAH
PERFECTION
PRECEPTS
PRIDE
PROMISE
REBELLION
RECONCILIATION
REDEMPTION
RIGHTEOUSNESS
SAYING
STATUTES
TABERNACLE
TEMPTATION
TESTIMONIES
TRANSGRESSION
VALUE
VENGEANCE
VICTORY
VINEYARD

WAY
WORD
WORSHIP

T	E	S	T	I	M	O	N	I	E	S	L	J	V	P
A	L	A	N	M	D	A	N	P	F	T	F	U	W	R
R	I	Y	D	W	O	R	D	E	C	A	A	D	I	E
I	Z	I	E	A	V	H	D	R	J	T	I	G	H	C
G	U	N	R	Y	E	T	I	F	Y	U	T	M	O	E
H	R	G	O	T	N	A	J	E	G	T	H	E	L	P
T	X	I	C	A	G	G	H	C	L	E	L	N	S	T
E	I	N	H	B	E	O	M	T	O	S	O	T	W	S
O	D	B	R	E	A	O	R	I	T	A	V	N	O	T
U	O	A	I	R	N	D	L	O	R	D	E	A	X	P
S	L	B	S	N	C	N	S	N	P	K	R	H	U	R
N	A	Y	T	A	E	E	M	E	S	S	I	A	H	O
E	T	L	R	C	I	S	S	I	T	V	F	O	L	M
S	R	O	N	L	E	S	O	M	E	I	A	N	I	I
S	Y	N	T	E	R	I	N	E	M	N	T	M	N	S
G	A	D	W	O	R	S	H	I	P	E	H	O	I	E
V	I	C	K	P	O	K	Y	C	T	Y	E	B	Q	U
I	H	E	G	V	A	L	U	E	A	A	R	Y	U	G
C	R	A	R	S	F	A	P	O	T	R	L	D	I	P
T	A	V	A	I	A	B	I	D	I	D	T	I	T	S
O	T	P	C	P	R	I	D	E	O	H	D	V	Y	T
R	E	D	E	M	P	T	I	O	N	P	H	I	N	W
Y	X	H	A	R	V	E	S	T	N	S	E	S	F	E
E	R	E	C	O	N	C	I	L	I	A	T	I	O	N
M	Y	R	E	B	E	L	L	I	O	N	R	O	L	V
T	R	A	N	S	G	R	E	S	S	I	O	N	L	E

WORD SEARCH – SHEET #10

DAVID
DAYS
DELIVERANCE
ELIJAH
FORTY
GOLIATH
HOREB
HUMILIATION
JEHOVAH
JESUS
JUDGES
JUSTICE
LAID
MEDIATOR
MT CARMEL
NIGHTS
PROBATION
RIGHTEOUS
RIVAL
SAINT
SALVATION
SAUL
SCRIPTURES
SERVITUDE
SIN
SOLOMON
SPIRIT
STRIPES   TROUBLES
TEMPTED   WORD
THIRTY   YEARS

```
S O L O M O N J O K D A V I D
A L E N M D I N J F A G R W S
U I N D A L G Y U C Y E A R S
L G J E R V H D S J S D A H A
E O A R T X T I T Y R M G O P
E L I J A H S J I G I E J L R
E I I E A O L H C L G D U S O
R A N S T R I P E S H I D W B
U T B U G A Q S P T T A G O A
T H G S E L G P H I E T E X T
E E B R A A H I R P O O S U I
M O S I N I U R A N U R H E O
P H A R K D T I B W S Y O L N
T R I N C P E T X I O N N I U
E E C D E L I V E R A N C E W
D A S E R V I T U D E N O B X
N I C K P O R I V A L E B P U
M T C A R M E L L N P W O R D
T J A N S A L V A T I O N R P
I E V U I A B S O M S A I N T
C H P M T H I R T Y H D F I W
H O N O K Y U A S W P H K N F
O V H U M I L I A T I O N F O
R A I S T R O U B L E S C A R
B A S C R I P T U R E S W L Y
```

WORD SEARCH – SHEET #11

WORDS BEGINNING WITH THE LETTER "W"

W	A	T	E	R	P	O	T	S	K	W	H	A	L	E
O	L	E	N	M	D	I	N	P	F	R	G	R	Y	S
R	I	N	D	W	A	L	L	S	C	E	E	A	X	S
M	W	O	R	M	V	H	D	U	J	A	D	A	E	A
W	O	N	D	E	R	F	U	L	Y	T	S	G	M	P
O	R	I	J	A	H	U	J	A	W	H	E	A	T	R
O	S	W	A	G	E	S	H	D	I	E	W	U	S	O
D	H	A	S	T	C	I	P	E	N	N	I	D	W	B
U	I	T	W	A	R	Q	R	P	T	A	Z	G	I	A
T	P	C	S	E	L	G	D	H	E	L	A	E	N	W
E	E	H	R	A	S	B	W	O	R	D	R	S	D	O
M	W	M	W	E	I	G	H	T	N	A	D	H	O	R
P	I	A	I	K	D	T	S	I	W	E	E	K	W	T
T	N	N	L	W	I	D	O	W	E	R	N	N	I	H
E	E	C	L	E	L	I	V	E	R	A	N	C	E	Y
H	B	S	O	B	W	I	F	E	W	E	N	O	B	X
S	I	C	W	R	I	T	E	V	I	L	E	B	P	U
S	B	C	O	P	N	E	W	L	N	P	W	I	N	D
E	B	A	L	S	E	W	H	O	N	W	O	O	L	P
N	E	V	F	I	A	I	I	S	O	I	M	I	O	W
R	R	P	M	T	H	D	S	S	W	S	A	F	I	E
E	Q	N	W	O	E	O	P	E	A	E	N	K	N	L
D	R	H	U	M	I	W	E	N	T	I	O	N	F	L
L	W	A	T	E	R	M	R	T	E	L	T	C	A	S
I	Y	R	W	Q	L	S	E	I	H	I	R	A	L	T
W	R	O	U	G	H	T	R	W	E	D	D	I	N	G

WAGES
WALLS
WAR
WATCHMAN
WATER
WATERPOTS
WEDDING
WEEK
WEIGHT
WELLS
WHALE
WHEAT
WHISPERER
WIDOW
WIDOWER
WIFE
WILDERNESS
WILLOW
WINDOW
WINE
WINEBIBBER
WINNOW
WINTER
WISE
WITNESS
WIZARD
WOE
WOLF
WOMAN
WONDERFUL
WOOL

WORD
WORM
WORMWOOD
WORSHIP
WREATH

WRITE
WROUGHT

WORD SEARCH – SHEET #12

ABISHAI
ABNER
ARMORBEARER
BATHSHEBA
BOAZ
COMMANDER
DEBORAH
ELI
GIDEON
GENERAL
JOAB
JONATHAN
KING
MERAB
MICHAL
MILLER
MUSICIAN
NAOMI
NATHAN
PIPERS
RELIGION
SAMSON
SAMUEL
SAUL
TEMPLE
TESTAMENT
THRONE
THUMMIM
TIBERIAS
URIAH
VASHNI
VILE

ZERUIAH
ZETHAM
ZETHAN
ZETHAR
ZIBA

```
B  O  A  Z  X  O  N  J  O  T  D  A  Z  I  N
A  L  E  N  M  D  I  O  P  I  E  G  V  W  A
T  I  U  D  A  L  G  A  B  B  B  E  A  R  O
H  G  J  R  R  V  H  B  Z  E  O  D  S  H  M
S  O  A  R  I  X  C  I  E  R  R  S  H  O  I
H  V  I  J  A  A  T  J  T  I  A  B  N  E  R
E  L  I  E  A  O  H  D  H  A  H  L  I  S  O
B  A  N  S  T  R  R  P  A  S  N  O  D  W  C
A  T  B  U  G  B  O  A  R  T  A  V  G  O  O
T  K  I  N  G  L  N  D  T  H  U  M  M  I  M
E  E  B  R  X  A  E  N  E  R  K  R  S  U  M
M  I  L  L  E  R  U  M  A  V  I  L  E  W  A
P  H  A  R  K  D  T  G  E  N  E  R  A  L  N
T  R  I  N  S  A  M  S  O  N  P  Q  N  I  D
E  E  C  M  U  S  I  C  I  A  N  N  Z  E  E
D  A  Z  E  R  U  I  A  H  D  E  N  I  B  R
N  A  T  H  A  N  R  I  V  A  L  E  B  P  U
P  Z  I  B  A  H  A  N  Z  E  T  H  A  N  A
I  E  A  N  S  F  A  T  E  M  P  L  E  Y  B
P  T  V  U  I  H  B  U  Z  Z  I  A  H  V  I
E  H  P  M  T  W  I  M  I  C  H  A  L  I  S
R  A  N  A  R  M  O  R  B  E  A  R  E  R  H
S  M  N  G  M  R  E  L  I  G  I  O  N  S  A
R  O  B  Y  H  A  M  E  R  A  B  T  C  A  I
J  T  E  S  T  A  M  E  N  T  I  R  A  U  T
P  G  I  D  E  O  N  X  S  A  M  U  E  L  Y
```

WORD SEARCH – SHEET #13

P	H	A	R	O	A	H	J	O	K	D	U	S	T	D
E	L	E	N	M	D	A	N	P	F	A	G	F	W	S
S	I	N	M	I	R	I	A	M	C	Y	E	R	R	S
T	G	J	E	R	V	L	I	V	E	S	T	O	C	K
I	O	A	F	A	M	I	N	E	Y	U	S	G	A	P
L	L	I	J	K	H	S	J	G	N	A	T	S	T	R
E	R	U	P	T	I	O	N	D	L	E	R	E	T	O
N	H	A	R	D	E	N	E	D	S	N	O	G	L	B
C	D	B	U	G	A	Q	R	P	T	A	N	Y	E	L
E	A	R	T	H	Q	U	A	K	E	S	G	P	X	O
E	R	L	R	A	K	H	S	R	P	A	R	T	U	C
M	K	E	U	P	I	N	P	A	N	N	S	I	E	U
P	N	P	G	K	U	T	S	I	W	D	Y	A	L	S
T	E	R	G	S	R	E	A	T	I	S	N	N	I	T
E	S	O	E	E	L	I	D	E	A	T	H	S	E	S
D	S	S	D	R	V	I	T	U	B	O	I	L	S	X
N	I	Y	K	A	A	R	O	N	A	R	E	B	P	U
I	S	R	A	E	L	I	T	E	S	M	W	O	R	D
T	R	A	N	S	F	J	P	O	P	S	T	A	F	F
S	A	V	O	L	C	A	N	O	M	I	N	I	O	L
E	G	Y	P	T	H	G	R	T	Y	H	D	F	I	I
R	Q	N	O	E	L	I	S	R	A	E	L	K	N	E
P	R	A	Y	E	R	S	I	A	T	I	O	N	F	S
E	L	I	S	H	A	W	A	T	E	R	T	C	A	R
N	Y	R	W	Q	L	S	T	A	B	L	O	O	D	Y
T	I	D	A	L	W	A	V	E	R	M	O	S	E	S

AARON
ASP
BLOODY
BOILS
CATTLE
DARKNESS
DEATH
DUST
EARTHQUAKES
EGYPT
EGYPTIANS
ERUPTION
FLIES
FROGS
GNATS
HAIL
ISRAEL
ISRAELITES
LEPROSY
LIVESTOCK
LOCUSTS
MIRIAM
MOSES
PESTILENCE
PHAROAH
PRAYERS
RUGGED
SANDSTORMS
SERPENT
STAFF
STRONG

SUN
TIDAL WAVE
VOLCANO
WATER

WORD SEARCH – SHEET #14

BOOK OF MARK

BAPTIZE		S	C	R	I	B	E	S	J	H	O	L	Y	V	F	C
BELIEVE		Y	L	E	N	A	D	P	N	P	F	A	G	R	O	A
CAMEL		N	I	N	D	P	L	I	Y	B	C	Y	E	A	R	P
CAPERNAUM		A	G	J	E	T	V	R	E	G	I	O	N	A	E	E
DEMONS		G	C	A	M	E	L	I	I	M	Y	E	S	G	R	R
DOCTRINE		O	L	I	J	Z	H	T	J	A	G	B	F	J	U	N
EUTHEOS		G	I	I	E	E	O	L	G	O	S	P	E	L	N	A
FISHERMAN		U	A	N	M	A	S	T	E	R	S	N	O	D	N	U
FORERUNNER		E	T	B	A	P	T	I	Z	E	T	A	V	G	E	M
GALILEAN		G	H	G	S	A	E	G	E	H	I	L	E	E	R	T
GODHEAD		O	E	B	C	R	S	H	B	E	L	I	E	V	E	P
GOSPEL		D	F	S	E	A	T	U	E	A	N	A	S	H	E	O
HEAVEN		H	I	A	R	B	I	T	D	O	C	T	R	I	N	E
HOLY		E	S	I	N	L	F	E	E	T	A	O	N	N	I	U
HUSBANDMEN		A	H	C	D	E	Y	I	E	E	M	A	N	C	E	S
LEPER		D	E	M	O	N	S	W	T	R	E	P	E	N	T	A
MASTER		N	R	C	K	A	O	R	I	V	L	L	E	B	P	B
MINISTRY		M	M	C	A	Z	G	A	L	I	L	E	A	N	R	B
NAZARETH		T	A	A	N	A	F	A	H	E	A	V	E	N	R	A
PARABLE		I	N	V	U	R	A	B	D	O	M	I	N	I	O	T
PRIEST		C	T	P	M	E	H	P	R	I	E	S	T	F	I	H
PROCLAIM		H	Q	S	A	T	A	N	A	E	U	T	H	E	O	S
REGION		O	R	H	U	H	U	S	B	A	N	D	M	E	N	O
REPENT		M	I	N	I	S	T	R	Y	M	E	L	E	P	E	R
SABBATH		E	Y	R	W	Q	L	S	P	R	O	C	L	A	I	M
SATAN		W	I	L	D	E	R	N	E	S	S	E	S	W	L	Y
SCRIBES		TESTIFY
SPIRIT		WILDERNESS
SYNAGOGUE		ZEBEDEE

WORD SEARCH – SHEET #15

BOOK OF PROVERBS

AUTHOR
DESPISE
DIDACTIC
DISCRETION
ENIGMA
EQUITY
FORSAKE
GRACEFUL
HOUSES
INNOCENT
INSTRUCTION
JUDGMENT
JUSTICE
KNOWLEDGE
PARALLELISM
PHILOSOPHER
POETICAL
POSSESSIONS
PRECIOUS
PROVERB
PRUDENCE
PURSE
SCIENTIST
SECTION
SHEOL
SINNERS
SOLOMON
SONGS
SPOIL
SWALLOW
VAIN
WALK

WISDOM
WISE
WONDER
WORDS
WORLD

D	I	S	C	R	E	T	I	O	N	D	W	A	L	K
E	L	P	N	E	Q	U	I	T	Y	A	G	R	W	N
S	I	O	P	H	I	L	O	S	O	P	H	E	R	O
P	G	I	E	R	V	W	U	S	W	A	L	L	O	W
I	O	L	R	T	X	O	I	M	I	E	S	G	O	L
S	L	I	J	A	H	R	J	U	S	B	O	J	L	E
E	N	I	G	M	A	D	H	D	D	E	L	U	S	D
R	A	N	R	T	R	S	P	E	O	N	O	D	W	G
Z	U	B	A	G	A	Q	R	P	M	A	M	G	O	E
Y	T	G	C	E	S	O	N	G	S	L	O	M	R	T
E	H	B	E	A	A	H	S	R	P	K	N	E	L	P
M	O	S	F	O	R	S	A	K	E	A	S	N	D	O
P	R	A	U	D	I	D	A	C	T	I	C	T	V	S
R	B	I	L	C	P	R	E	C	I	O	U	S	J	S
U	W	C	D	E	D	I	V	E	P	A	N	E	U	E
D	O	S	I	N	N	E	R	S	D	E	N	C	S	S
E	N	C	K	P	R	O	V	E	R	B	E	K	T	S
N	D	C	S	H	E	O	L	M	N	P	W	O	I	I
C	E	V	U	G	A	W	I	S	E	U	N	I	C	O
E	R	S	C	I	E	N	T	I	S	T	K	P	E	N
C	T	P	A	R	A	L	L	E	L	I	S	M	I	S
H	O	U	S	E	S	I	A	S	A	P	H	K	N	F
O	R	R	U	M	I	N	N	O	C	E	N	T	F	V
R	L	S	P	O	E	T	I	C	A	L	T	C	A	A
E	Y	E	W	Q	L	D	S	E	C	T	I	O	N	I
I	N	S	T	R	U	C	T	I	O	N	S	W	L	N

WORD SEARCH – SHEET #16

THE BOOK OF EPHESIANS

ABOUND
APOSTLE
BELOVED
BLESSED
CHRIST
CHRISTIAN
DISPENSATION
DOMINION
EPHESUS
FORGIVENESS
FOUNDATION
FULLNESS
GLORY
GRACE
GREATNESS
HEAVEN
INHERITANCE
POWER
PRAYER
PREDESTINED
PRINCIPALITY
REDEMPTION
REVELATION
RIGHTEOUSNESS
SAINT
SALVATION
SPIRITUAL
STRENGTH
SUFFICIENT
TESTING
TRANSFORM
UNDERSTANDING
UNMERITED
WORLD
WORTHY

```
U N D E R S T A N D I N G I F
A C U P E T I B P R N G R W O
F H N H D R G O B I H E E R U
O R M E E E H U U G E B V B N
R I E S M N T N M H R L E E D
G S R U P G W D E T I E L L A
I T I S T T L H D E T S A O T
V I T M I H I P E O A S T V I
E A E W O R T H Y U N E I E O
N N D S N L G D H S C D O D N
E A P O S T L E R N E R N F W
S O S E P I U M A E A S W U S
S P I R I T U A L S S Y P L A
T R I N G L O R Y S O N R L I
H E S U F F I C I E N T A N N
E D S E C H R I S T E N Y E T
A E C K P O R I V A L E E S U
V S A L V A T I O N P W R S W
E T V U I A D O M I N I O N O
N I T R A N S F O R M L A S R
C N X M R H I R T Y H D F I L
H E Y E E T E S T I N G K G D
O D W C H R I I A T I O N R O
R O G R E A T N E S S T C A R
P R I N C I P A L I T Y A C T
D I S P E N S A T I O N W E Y
```

WORD SEARCH – SHEET #17

A	N	O	I	N	T	I	N	G	K	D	R	I	N	K
T	L	E	N	M	D	I	N	P	F	E	S	R	W	I
O	I	C	U	R	T	A	I	N	C	F	A	A	C	N
N	G	J	O	R	V	H	D	U	L	I	C	A	I	S
E	O	I	R	T	X	T	I	M	E	L	R	G	R	M
M	L	I	J	A	H	S	J	A	R	E	I	J	C	E
E	I	I	E	B	L	O	O	D	G	M	F	U	U	N
N	A	V	E	N	G	E	R	U	Y	E	I	B	M	B
T	T	B	U	G	A	Q	R	P	L	N	C	R	C	C
W	I	S	D	O	M	G	D	H	I	T	I	E	I	A
O	E	C	E	R	E	M	O	N	Y	K	A	A	S	L
R	O	S	E	P	I	U	M	A	N	A	L	S	I	F
D	H	C	H	I	E	F	P	R	I	E	S	T	O	N
I	R	I	C	O	M	M	U	N	I	O	N	P	N	B
N	C	L	E	A	N	L	I	N	E	S	S	L	P	A
A	A	S	E	R	E	I	T	U	D	Y	N	A	R	A
N	I	C	K	R	O	R	I	V	A	L	E	T	E	L
C	O	N	G	R	E	G	A	T	I	O	N	E	A	D
E	R	E	L	A	T	I	O	N	S	H	I	P	C	P
I	A	P	E	N	T	E	C	O	S	T	N	I	H	N
F	B	L	E	S	S	I	N	G	B	H	D	F	E	T
E	Q	N	O	E	P	H	Y	L	A	C	T	E	R	Y
A	L	T	A	R	I	L	I	A	T	I	O	M	F	O
S	L	C	O	M	M	U	N	I	T	Y	U	C	A	R
T	Y	R	F	R	E	E	W	I	L	L	R	A	R	K
S	A	E	P	H	O	D	T	I	N	C	E	N	S	E

ALTAR
ANOINTING
ARK
ATONEMENT
AVENGER
BAAL
BLESSING
BLOOD
BREASTPLATE
CALF
CEREMONY
CHIEF PRIEST
CIRCUMCISION
CLEANLINESS
CLERGY
COMMUNION
COMMUNITY
CONGREGATION
CURTAIN
DEFILEMENT
DRINK
EPHOD
FEASTS
FREEWILL
HOLY
INCENSE
KINSMEN
OIL
ORDINANCE
PENTECOST
PHYLACTERY
PREACHER
RELATIONSHIP
RULER
SACRIFICIAL
SOUL
WISDOM

WORD SEARCH – SHEET #18

BLESS
CHURCH
CHRIST
CORONATION
DEACON
ELDERS
EVANGELIST
EXCOMMUNICATION
FELLOWSHIP
GENTILE
GREEK
HOLY
HUMANITY
HYMN
JESUS
JEW
JUDAISM
LEADER
MISSIONARY
ORDINATION
OVERSEER
PHARISEE
SACREMENT
SADDUCEE
SANHEDRIN
SAMARITAN
SANCTUARY
SECT
SEER
SHRINE
SONG

TABLET
TEACHER
TETRACH
VICTORY

```
E  X  C  O  M  M  U  N  I  C  A  T  I  O  N
V  L  E  S  I  D  I  B  L  E  S  S  R  R  S
A  I  N  O  S  A  C  R  E  M  E  N  T  D  A
N  G  A  N  S  I  T  I  M  Y  E  S  G  I  N
G  E  J  G  I  L  E  L  D  E  R  S  P  N  H
E  N  L  C  O  T  L  H  Y  M  N  L  I  A  E
L  T  E  N  N  V  J  U  D  A  I  S  M  T  D
I  I  A  W  A  O  I  P  E  S  N  O  C  I  R
S  L  D  P  R  K  Q  G  R  E  E  K  T  O  I
T  E  E  U  Y  L  D  E  A  C  O  N  O  N  N
E  C  R  V  I  C  T  O  R  Y  K  R  V  U  E
O  O  S  S  A  M  A  R  I  T  A  N  S  P  O
V  R  A  R  S  E  C  T  I  W  S  P  B  H  N
E  O  R  N  C  R  T  E  T  R  A  C  H  A  U
R  N  A  D  E  L  I  V  E  L  A  V  J  R  S
S  A  D  D  U  C  E  E  A  D  J  N  T  I  H
E  T  I  K  P  O  R  I  C  A  E  E  A  S  E
E  I  A  A  R  M  E  L  H  N  S  W  B  E  P
R  O  N  H  O  L  Y  P  E  P  U  C  L  E  H
I  N  T  U  I  A  B  D  R  M  S  H  E  O  E
C  S  A  N  C  T  U  A  R  Y  H  R  T  I  R
H  Q  N  O  E  C  H  U  R  C  H  I  K  N  D
O  R  H  U  M  A  N  I  T  Y  I  S  N  F  O
R  L  I  S  H  R  I  N  E  E  L  T  C  A  R
E  Y  R  W  Q  S  E  E  R  H  I  R  A  L  T
F  E  L  L  O  W  S  H  I  P  E  S  J  E  W
```

98

WORD SEARCH – SHEET #19

ABIJAH
ANGEL
BARREN
CLEAN
COMMANDMENTS
CONCEIVE
COUSINS
DAY SPRING
DISOBEDIENT
ELIZABETH
EXCELLENT
EYEWITNESSES
FAVOR
GABRIEL
GLAD TIDINGS
GOOD WORKS
HEART
HEROD
HOLY SPIRIT
JESUS
JOHN
LAW
MINISTRY
PREACH
PRIESTHOOD
PROMISE
PULPIT
SOCIAL
SUFFER
THEOPHILUS

VICTORY
ZACHARIAS

A	B	I	J	A	H	P	E	G	V	D	R	I	N	Z
T	L	E	N	M	D	W	S	P	I	I	P	R	W	A
O	I	C	O	U	S	I	N	S	C	S	R	E	C	C
C	Z	J	E	S	U	S	D	U	T	O	I	X	I	H
O	O	A	R	H	E	A	R	T	O	B	E	C	R	A
M	I	N	I	S	T	R	Y	A	R	E	S	E	C	R
M	N	I	E	X	L	U	O	D	Y	D	T	L	U	I
A	A	V	C	N	G	E	R	E	U	I	H	L	D	A
N	G	O	O	D	W	O	R	K	S	E	O	E	A	S
D	Y	G	N	E	L	G	D	H	I	N	O	N	Y	C
M	A	C	C	R	E	M	O	N	Y	T	D	T	S	A
E	H	L	E	P	R	E	A	C	H	A	S	S	P	L
N	O	R	I	I	G	F	P	H	L	E	F	T	R	F
T	L	I	V	C	P	U	L	P	I	T	A	P	I	D
S	Y	L	E	A	N	L	I	N	E	S	V	W	N	B
A	S	U	F	F	E	R	W	V	X	E	O	H	G	A
N	P	C	K	P	O	W	E	R	C	L	R	R	P	R
C	I	N	G	R	H	C	A	U	P	O	N	E	R	R
E	R	I	A	S	E	A	P	R	O	M	I	S	E	E
I	I	P	B	N	R	E	C	O	S	T	N	I	O	N
F	T	P	R	S	O	C	I	A	L	H	T	W	Y	K
E	Q	N	I	E	D	L	V	L	A	O	J	O	H	N
A	N	G	E	L	I	E	L	I	Z	A	B	E	T	H
S	L	C	L	G	L	A	D	T	I	D	I	N	G	S
E	Y	E	W	I	T	N	E	S	S	E	S	A	R	K
T	H	E	O	P	H	I	L	U	S	C	E	L	A	W

99

WORD SEARCH – SHEET #20

ADORATION
AMEN
BENEDICTION
CHALLENGE
COMMEMORATION
COMMEND
CONFESSION
DECISION
DOXOLOGY
EDIFICATION
ENCOURAGEMENT
ENDURANCE
ENLIGHTENMENT
EQUIPMENT
EVANGELISM
GIVING
GLORIFY
GRACE
GROWTH
HAPPY
HEART
HONOR
HOSPITALITY
HYMNAL
LAUGH
LOVE
MEDITATION
MERCY
PERSEVERANCE
PRAISE

PRAY
PRIORITY
REJOICE
STUDY

TESTIFY
TESTIMONY
THANKSGIVING

T	B	C	A	D	O	R	A	T	I	O	N	P	C	E
H	Q	O	H	X	G	R	A	C	E	F	B	E	O	N
A	Z	N	Y	C	O	M	M	E	N	D	U	R	M	L
N	D	F	M	R	W	C	G	L	P	X	Y	S	M	I
K	O	E	N	E	J	P	R	A	I	S	E	E	E	G
S	X	S	A	J	M	R	X	R	G	W	N	V	M	H
G	O	S	L	O	G	I	V	I	N	G	D	E	O	T
I	L	I	F	I	H	O	N	O	R	O	U	R	R	E
V	O	O	R	C	T	R	G	N	H	B	R	A	A	N
I	G	N	Q	E	V	I	F	A	A	E	A	N	T	M
N	Y	W	P	J	P	T	L	M	P	N	N	C	I	E
G	L	O	R	I	F	Y	A	E	P	E	C	E	O	N
S	K	C	O	H	R	C	X	N	Y	D	E	T	N	T
E	V	U	I	M	E	R	C	Y	P	I	M	E	D	Y
Q	T	R	S	W	Q	X	H	K	L	C	E	D	M	E
U	W	D	E	C	I	S	I	O	N	T	N	I	E	V
I	O	V	I	H	E	A	R	T	R	I	T	F	D	A
P	R	A	Y	A	K	L	O	P	W	O	T	I	I	N
M	S	Z	O	L	A	U	G	H	Z	N	E	C	T	G
E	H	C	P	L	O	V	E	S	B	V	S	A	A	E
N	I	I	M	E	D	S	T	U	D	Y	T	T	T	L
T	P	X	J	N	C	X	V	B	P	J	I	I	I	I
W	L	E	D	G	R	O	W	T	H	I	F	O	O	S
I	Z	R	T	E	S	T	I	M	O	N	Y	N	N	M
H	O	S	P	I	T	A	L	I	T	Y	P	M	E	R
E	N	C	O	U	R	A	G	E	M	E	N	T	W	C

WORD SEARCH – SHEET #21

ASSURANCE	S	P	I	R	I	T	U	A	L	K	D	R	I	N	D
CELEBRATION	p	L	E	N	M	D	I	N	O	F	E	G	R	W	E
DENIAL	K	R	E	L	I	G	I	O	N	C	F	L	I	F	T
DETERMINATION	F	G	J	E	R	V	H	D	G	J	I	D	X	I	E
DISCIPLINE	S	E	L	F	S	A	C	R	I	F	I	C	E	J	R
EXAMINATION	A	S	S	U	R	A	N	C	E	G	E	F	G	C	M
FRIENDSHIP	R	T	W	E	E	L	O	O	D	L	M	L	U	U	I
GUIDANCE	E	R	A	W	F	R	I	E	N	D	S	H	I	P	N
INQUIRE	C	I	R	H	O	I	R	R	P	I	W	V	D	C	A
JUST	L	V	F	O	R	G	E	D	H	S	O	E	A	I	T
LIFT	A	E	A	L	M	H	S	O	N	C	N	R	N	N	I
LONG	I	O	R	E	A	T	P	M	A	I	D	S	C	Q	O
PROGRESS	M	H	E	S	T	E	O	P	R	P	E	R	E	U	N
RECLAIM	P	W	T	O	I	O	N	R	E	L	R	E	V	I	B
REFORMATION	W	I	H	M	O	U	S	O	N	I	F	S	A	R	R
RELIGION	A	T	E	E	N	S	I	G	E	N	U	P	L	E	E
REMEMBER	T	H	O	K	P	N	B	R	W	E	L	E	U	P	M
RENEWAL	C	S	L	G	R	E	L	E	A	I	O	C	A	R	E
RENUNCIATION	H	T	O	N	S	S	E	S	L	P	U	T	B	R	M
RESPECT	F	A	G	E	N	S	J	S	O	S	Z	N	L	O	B
RESPONSIBLE	U	N	Y	M	T	H	I	R	T	I	T	H	E	J	E
RIGHTEOUSNESS	L	D	N	O	E	P	D	E	N	I	A	L	E	U	R
SELF-SACRIFICE	N	C	E	L	E	B	R	A	T	I	O	N	N	S	O
SPIRITUAL	E	X	A	M	I	N	A	T	I	O	N	U	C	T	R
STRIVE	S	Y	R	F	R	E	E	K	W	I	T	N	E	S	S
THEOLOGY	S	R	E	N	U	N	C	I	A	T	I	O	N	S	E
TITHE
VALUABLE	WHOLESOME		WONDERFUL
WARFARE	WITHSTAND
WATCHFULNESS	WITNESS

WORD SEARCH – SHEET #22

AFFLUENCE
APOSTASY
ASTOLOGY
ATHEISM
DECEPTION
DISCOURAGEMENT
DISHONESTY
DISOBEDIENCE
DISTRUST
DOUBT
ENEMY
ENVY
EVIL
FAILURE
FAITHLESSNESS
FAVORITISM
FOLLY
FOOLS
GRUDGE
LEGALISM
LIBERTINISM
LIES
LUST
MATERIALISM
MOCKERY
NEGLECT

D	L	I	B	E	R	T	I	N	I	S	M	I	N	F
I	I	E	N	M	D	I	N	P	E	E	G	R	W	A
S	I	S	U	F	T	A	I	N	C	G	E	A	C	V
O	G	J	C	R	O	H	D	U	J	R	L	A	I	O
B	O	A	R	O	X	O	I	M	Y	U	S	E	R	R
E	L	I	J	A	U	S	L	A	Z	D	F	J	C	I
D	I	I	E	T	L	R	O	S	L	G	L	U	U	T
I	A	J	E	H	F	E	A	S	E	O	B	M	I
E	V	I	L	E	A	Q	F	G	T	N	V	R	C	S
N	H	G	E	I	I	G	F	H	E	T	E	E	I	M
C	E	C	G	S	L	M	L	N	Y	M	R	A	S	C
E	O	S	A	M	U	K	U	A	N	A	E	S	I	L
D	H	C	L	I	R	Y	E	R	I	E	S	N	O	I
I	R	I	I	C	E	W	N	T	I	O	N	A	T	E
N	C	L	S	E	N	L	C	N	E	S	S	P	E	S
A	A	S	M	R	V	I	E	U	D	E	N	O	Z	A
N	I	C	K	D	I	S	T	R	U	S	T	S	P	D
C	O	N	G	A	S	T	O	L	O	G	Y	T	E	I
M	A	T	E	R	I	A	L	I	S	M	L	A	N	S
I	A	P	K	N	T	E	C	M	S	D	N	S	E	H
F	T	D	E	C	E	P	T	I	O	N	D	Y	M	O
E	Q	N	O	Y	P	H	Y	U	A	C	T	E	Y	N
A	J	T	L	R	I	L	B	A	T	I	K	N	F	E
S	X	L	U	M	M	T	B	I	T	Y	U	E	A	S
T	O	R	S	R	E	N	V	Y	C	F	R	A	R	T
F	A	I	T	H	L	E	S	S	N	E	S	S	W	Y

WORD SEARCH – SHEET #23

BLAMELESSNESS
BOLDNESS
CHARACTER
CHASTITY
CHILDLIKENESS
CHRIST
COMMITMENT
CONFIDENCE
CONFORMITY
CONSECRATION
COURAGE
DEDICATION
DEPENDENCE
DEVOTION
DISCERN
DISCIPLINE
DOCTRINE
EARNESTNESS
ETHICS
FAITHFULNESS
FRUITFULNESS
GENTLENESS
GODLINESS
HOLINESS
HONESTY
HUMILITY
LOYAL
STAUNCH
UNERRING

B	L	A	M	E	L	E	S	S	N	E	S	S	N	K
O	L	E	N	A	D	E	V	O	T	I	O	N	F	I
L	I	C	U	R	T	A	D	N	C	F	E	R	A	N
D	G	H	E	N	V	H	O	U	J	I	D	A	I	S
N	O	R	D	E	D	I	C	A	T	I	O	N	T	M
E	L	I	S	S	H	S	T	A	G	E	F	J	H	E
S	C	S	T	T	L	O	R	D	L	M	L	U	F	F
S	H	T	A	N	G	E	I	E	S	E	O	B	U	R
T	A	B	U	E	A	Q	N	P	T	N	C	R	L	U
D	S	G	N	S	L	G	E	H	I	C	O	G	N	I
E	T	C	C	S	E	M	O	N	M	O	M	E	E	T
P	I	C	H	D	I	S	C	E	R	N	M	N	S	F
E	T	H	I	C	S	F	P	R	I	F	I	T	S	U
N	Y	I	H	O	N	E	S	T	Y	I	T	L	O	L
D	C	L	C	A	N	L	I	N	L	D	M	E	E	N
E	A	D	O	U	V	I	T	A	C	E	E	N	D	E
N	H	L	N	N	O	R	Y	V	O	N	N	E	I	S
C	O	I	F	E	E	O	A	T	U	C	T	S	S	S
E	L	K	O	R	L	A	P	O	R	E	L	S	C	P
I	I	E	R	R	T	E	C	O	A	T	N	I	I	N
F	N	N	M	I	H	I	R	T	G	H	D	F	P	T
E	E	E	I	N	P	H	Y	L	E	C	T	E	L	Y
A	S	S	T	G	O	D	L	I	N	E	S	S	I	O
W	S	S	Y	M	H	U	M	I	L	I	T	Y	N	R
T	Y	R	F	R	E	C	H	A	R	A	C	T	E	R
C	O	N	S	E	C	R	E	T	I	O	N	N	S	E

WORD SEARCH – SHEET #24

T	R	E	V	E	R	E	N	C	E	X	N	W	J	M
R	E	C	A	L	M	N	E	S	S	B	U	A	H	O
U	C	W	Z	L	O	Y	A	L	T	Y	R	R	C	D
S	E	R	E	S	T	R	A	I	N	T	T	M	V	E
T	P	E	R	C	E	P	T	I	O	N	U	T	P	R
W	T	Y	S	R	T	A	L	O	V	E	R	H	K	N
O	I	F	G	E	I	T	Q	U	A	G	E	J	I	A
R	V	O	X	C	M	I	F	S	E	R	V	A	N	T
T	E	R	F	G	O	E	I	A	V	N	H	W	D	I
H	V	B	H	M	D	N	P	I	E	T	Y	N	O
Y	P	E	R	F	E	C	T	I	O	N	P	M	E	N
W	U	A	E	O	S	E	O	S	R	G	D	E	S	X
O	R	R	A	R	T	R	L	T	T	E	Y	E	S	M
R	I	A	D	T	Y	E	E	O	H	N	S	K	G	E
S	T	N	I	I	B	L	R	I	O	T	S	N	O	R
H	Y	C	N	T	D	I	A	C	D	L	E	E	O	C
I	N	E	E	U	F	S	N	I	O	E	P	S	D	I
P	D	X	S	D	J	H	C	S	X	H	A	S	W	F
U	P	T	S	E	C	B	E	M	Y	J	R	B	I	U
M	O	R	A	L	I	T	Y	P	O	K	A	D	L	L
Y	Q	Z	X	Y	I	N	S	I	G	H	T	M	L	N
A	D	O	R	A	T	I	O	N	V	W	I	F	R	E
R	E	L	I	A	B	L	E	Y	S	X	O	K	W	S
V	I	R	T	U	E	Q	U	I	E	T	N	E	S	S
W	A	R	M	H	E	A	R	T	E	D	N	E	S	S
I	N	N	O	C	E	N	C	E	F	G	X	J	O	Y

ADORATION
CALMNESS
FORBEARANCE
FORTITUDE
GENTLE
GOODWILL
INNOCENCE
INSIGHT
INTOLERANCE
JOY
KINDNESS
LOVE
LOYALTY
MEEKNESS
MERCIFULNESS
MODERNATION
MODESTY
MORALITY
NURTURE
ORTHODOXY
PATIENCE
PERCEPTION
PERFECTION
PIETY
PURITY
QUIETNESS
READINESS
RECEPTIVE
RELIABLE
RELISH

RESTRAINT
REVERENCE
SEPARATION
SERVANT

STOICISM
TRUSTWORTHY
VIRTUE
WARMHEARTEDNESS

WARMTH
WORSHIP

WORD SEARCH – SHEET #25

F	I	D	O	L	A	T	R	Y	K	F	G	P	H	U
O	P	P	R	E	S	S	I	O	N	L	B	O	C	N
R	X	M	H	Y	P	O	C	R	I	S	Y	L	W	F
G	J	Q	X	S	H	A	M	E	F	U	L	Y	V	O
E	P	E	R	S	E	C	U	T	I	O	N	T	O	R
T	Y	J	E	A	L	O	U	S	L	Y	R	H	P	G
F	O	R	G	I	V	E	N	E	S	S	D	E	P	I
U	N	S	E	L	F	I	S	H	I	K	P	I	O	V
L	V	T	P	R	E	M	O	R	S	E	F	S	S	E
N	H	U	N	G	R	A	T	E	F	U	L	M	I	N
E	P	R	E	S	U	M	P	T	I	O	N	J	T	E
S	K	E	M	P	A	T	H	Y	H	D	B	W	I	S
S	U	P	E	R	S	T	I	T	I	O	N	O	O	S
G	N	B	M	E	U	H	G	M	V	P	C	R	N	J
U	D	Y	E	J	S	A	K	W	F	Z	A	T	C	H
W	E	S	E	U	P	N	I	C	E	G	R	H	P	E
O	R	P	K	D	I	K	N	O	Y	U	E	I	H	R
R	S	I	N	I	C	F	D	G	V	I	X	N	C	E
L	T	T	E	C	I	U	N	B	E	L	I	E	F	S
D	A	E	S	E	O	L	K	J	D	T	K	S	O	Y
L	N	F	S	Z	N	B	R	W	I	S	E	S	L	M
I	D	U	W	Q	P	R	I	D	E	U	V	T	L	I
N	I	L	V	U	L	G	A	R	I	T	Y	P	Y	F
E	N	D	C	O	N	S	C	I	E	N	C	E	G	E
S	G	K	J	I	D	G	E	N	E	R	O	U	S	A
S	L	O	T	H	F	U	L	N	E	S	S	W	I	R

CARE
CONSCIENCE
EMPATHY
FEAR
FOLLY
FORGETFULNESS
FORGIVENESS
GENEROUS
GRATEFUL
GUILT
HERESY
IDOLATRY
JEALOUSLY
MEEKNESS
NICE
OPPRESSION
OPPOSITION
PERSECUTION
POLYTHEISM
PREJUDICE
PRESUMPTION
PRIDE
REMORSE
SHAMEFUL
SLOTHFULNESS
SPITEFUL
SUSPICION
SUPERSTITION
THANKFUL
UNBELIEF
UNDERSTANDING
UNFORGIVENESS
UNSELFISH
VULGARITY
WISE
WORLDLINESS
WORTHINESS

WHO SAID THAT?

WHO SAID THAT?
OLD TESTAMENT – SHEET #1

Read each statement then identify the speaker by circling A, B, C, or D. Statements are taken from Old and New Testament scriptures.

1. "Please feed me with that same red stew, for I am weary."

A.	Jacob	C.	Adam
B.	Elijah	D.	Esau

2. "Please tell me where your great strength lies, and with what you may be bound to afflict you."

A.	Hannah	C.	Delilah
B.	Sarah	D.	Deborah

3. "It is good, my daughter, that you go out with his young women, and that people do not meet you in any other field."

A.	Esther	C.	Anna
B.	Ruth	D.	Naomi

4. "Do not look at his appearance or at his physical stature, because I have refused him. For the Lord does not see as man sees; for man looks at the outward appearance, but the Lord looks at the heart."

A.	The Lord	C.	Elimelech
B.	Samuel	D.	Jonathan

5. "God is my strength and power; And He makes my way perfect."

A.	David	C.	Abishai
B.	Saul	D.	Joab

WHO SAID THAT?
OLD TESTAMENT – SHEET #2
Read each statement then identify the speaker by circling A, B, C, or D. Statements are taken from Old and New Testament scriptures.

1. "Arise, anoint him; for this is the one!"

   A. _____ Saul   C. _____ Lamech
   B. _____ The Lord   D. _____ Jesse

2. "Look, I have seen a son of Jesse the Bethlehemite, who is skillful in playing, a mighty man of valor, a man of war, prudent in speech, and a handsome person; and the LORD is with him."

   A. _____ Abinadab   C. _____ A Servant
   B. _____ Shammah   D. _____ Eliab

3. "Man who is born of woman Is of few days and full of trouble."

   A. _____ Job   C. _____ The Lord
   B. _____ Satan   D. _____ Isaac

4. "It is good and fitting for one to eat and drink, and to enjoy the good of all his labor in which he toils under the sun all the days of his life which God gives him; for it is his heritage."

   A. _____ Samuel   C. _____ Sarah
   B. _____ Solomon   D. _____ Shammah

5. "Of all that I said to the woman let her be careful. She may not eat anything that comes from the vine, nor may she drink wine or similar drink, nor eat anything unclean. All that I commanded her let her observe."

   A. _____ Angel of the Lord   C. _____ Moses
   B. _____ Gabriel   D. _____ Joshua

WHO SAID THAT?
OLD TESTAMENT – SHEET #3

Read each statement then identify the speaker by circling A, B, C, or D. Statements are taken from Old and New Testament scriptures.

1. "We shall surely die, because we have seen God!"

   A. _____ David _____   C. _____ Manoah _____
   B. _____ Elijah _____   D. _____ Absalom _____

2. "I will now turn aside and see this great sight, why the bush does not burn."

   A. _____ Joshua _____   C. _____ Noah _____
   B. _____ Moses _____   D. _____ Aaron _____

3. "Do not draw near this place. Take your sandals off your feet, for the place where you stand *is* holy ground."

   A. _____ The Lord _____   C. _____ King David _____
   B. _____ King Josiah _____   D. _____ King Solomon _____

4. "I AM WHO I AM."

   A. _____ Christ _____   C. _____ Joseph _____
   B. _____ God _____   D. _____ Pharoah _____

5. "Do not be afraid. Stand still, and see the salvation of the LORD, which He will accomplish for you today."

   A. _____ Noah _____   C. _____ Levi _____
   B. _____ Shem _____   D. _____ Moses _____

WHO SAID THAT?
OLD TESTAMENT – SHEET #4

Read each statement then identify the speaker by circling A, B, C, or D. Statements are taken from Old and New Testament scriptures.

1. "Yes, the men came to me, but I did not know where they were from. And it happened as the gate was being shut, when it was dark, that the men went out. Where the men went, I do not know; pursue them quickly, for you may overtake them."

A.	Lydia	C.	Rahab
B.	Tamar	D.	Susanna

2. "My son, I beg you, give glory to the LORD God of Israel, and make confession to Him, and tell me now what you have done; do not hide it from me."

A.	Aaron	C.	Joshua
B.	Moses	D.	Jethro

3. "Indeed I have sinned against the LORD God of Israel, and this is what I have done: When I saw among the spoils a beautiful Babylonian garment, two hundred shekels of silver, and a wedge of gold weighing fifty shekels, I coveted them and took them. And there they are, hidden in the earth in the midst of my tent, with the silver under it."

A.	Zerah	C.	Zabdi
B.	Achan	D.	Caleb

4. "Why have you troubled us? The LORD will trouble you this day."

A.	Moses	C.	Miriam
B.	Abraham	D.	Joshua

5. "Woe is me, for I am undone! Because I am a man of unclean lips, And I dwell in the midst of a people of unclean lips; For my eyes have seen the King, The LORD of hosts."

A.	Hosea	C.	Isaiah
B.	Joshua	D.	Jeremiah

WHO SAID THAT?
OLD TESTAMENT – SHEET #5

Read each statement then identify the speaker by circling A, B, C, or D. Statements are taken from Old and New Testament scriptures.

1. "Behold, this has touched your lips; Your iniquity is taken away, And your sin purged."

A.	God	C.	A Seraphim
B.	Aaron	D.	Moses

2. "Whom shall I send, And who will go for Us?"

A.	Joshua	C.	Gabriel
B.	The Lord	D.	Moses

3. For unto us a Child is born, Unto us a Son is given; And the government will be upon His shoulder. And His name will be called Wonderful, Counselor, Mighty God, Everlasting Father, Prince of Peace."

A.	Isaiah	C.	Chief Priests
B.	God	D.	Zipporah

4. "The wolf also shall dwell with the lamb, The leopard shall lie down with the young goat, The calf and the young lion and the fatling together; And a little child shall lead them."

A.	God	C.	Aaron
B.	Isaiah	D.	Abraham

5. "And in that day there shall be a Root of Jesse, Who shall stand as a banner to the people; For the Gentiles shall seek Him, And His resting place shall be glorious."

A.	King Ahaz	C.	Isaiah
B.	King Solomon	D.	God

WHO SAID THAT?
OLD TESTAMENT – SHEET #6
Read each statement then identify the speaker by circling A, B, C, or D. Statements are taken from Old and New Testament scriptures.

1. "The woman whom You gave to be with me, she gave me of the tree, and I ate."

A.	Adam	C.	Seth
B.	Moses	D.	Cain

2. "The serpent deceived me, and I ate."

A.	Martha	C.	Eve
B.	Salome	D.	Sarah

3. "Behold, the man has become like one of Us, to know good and evil. And now, lest he put out his hand and take also of the tree of life, and eat, and live forever."

A.	The Lord God	C.	King Darius
B.	Samuel	D.	Scribes

4. "...Am I my brother's keeper?"

A.	Cain	C.	Ham
B.	Abel	D.	Jephthah

5. "Cursed be Canaan; A servant of servants He shall be to his brethren."

A.	God	C.	Job
B.	Noah	D.	David

WHO SAID THAT?
OLD TESTAMENT – SHEET #7

Read each statement then identify the speaker by circling A, B, C, or D. Statements are taken from Old and New Testament scriptures.

1. "I will bless those who bless you, And I will curse him who curses you; And in you all the families of the earth shall be blessed."

A.	The Lord	C.	Joshua
B.	Aaron	D.	Gideon

2. "Lift your eyes now and look from the place where you are—northward, southward, eastward, and westward; for all the land which you see I give to you and your descendants forever."

A.	The Lord	C.	Abraham
B.	Lot	D.	Moses

3. "Blessed be Abram of God Most High, Possessor of heaven and earth; And blessed be God Most High, Who has delivered your enemies into your hand."

A.	Melchizedek	C.	King of Gomorrah
B.	King of Sodom	D.	Arioch King of Ellasar

4. "My wrong *be* upon you! I gave my maid into your embrace; and when she saw that she had conceived, I became despised in her eyes. The LORD judge between you and me."

A.	Sarai	C.	Rebekah
B.	Rachel	D.	Keturah

5. "Behold, you are with child, And you shall bear a son. You shall call his name Ishmael, Because the LORD has heard your affliction."

A.	Angel of the Lord	C.	Aaron
B.	Joshua	D.	Moses

WHO SAID THAT?
OLD TESTAMENT – SHEET #8

Read each statement then identify the speaker by circling A, B, C, or D. Statements are taken from Old and New Testament scriptures.

1. "Why did Sarah laugh, saying, 'Shall I surely bear a child, since I am old?'

A.	The Lord	C.	Nahor
B.	Lot	D.	Lamech

2. "If I find in Sodom fifty righteous within the city, then I will spare all the place for their sakes."

A.	Sarah	C.	Zipporah
B.	The Lord	D.	Miriam

3. "Here now, my lords, please turn in to your servant's house and spend the night and wash your feet; then you may rise early and go on your way."

A.	Abraham	C.	Shem
B.	Lot	D.	Laban

4. "Escape for your life! Do not look behind you nor stay anywhere in the plain. Escape to the mountains, lest you be destroyed."

A.	Haran	C.	One of the Angels
B.	Aaron	D.	Moses

5. Come, let us make our father drink wine, and we will lie with him, that we may preserve the lineage of our father."

A.	Lot's First-born Daughter	C.	Esther
B.	Lot's Youngest Daughter	D.	Ruth

WHO SAID THAT?
OLD TESTAMENT – SHEET #9

Read each statement then identify the speaker by circling A, B, C, or D. Statements are taken from Old and New Testament scriptures.

1. "The righteous will never be removed, But the wicked will not inhabit the earth."

A.	Solomon	C.	David
B.	Isaiah	D.	Angel of the Lord

2. "Though your sins are like scarlet, They shall be as white as snow; Though they are red like crimson, They shall be as wool. If you are willing and obedient, You shall eat the good of the land; But if you refuse and rebel, You shall be devoured by the sword;"

A.	Gideon	C.	Jerubbaal
B.	The Lord	D.	Jothan

3. "With the jawbone of a donkey, Heaps upon heaps, With the jawbone of a donkey I have slain a thousand men!"

A.	Saul	C.	Samson
B.	Gideon	D.	Samuel

4. "Entreat me not to leave you, *Or to* turn back from following after you; For wherever you go, I will go; And wherever you lodge, I will lodge; Your people shall be my people, And your God, my God. Where you die, I will die, And there will I be buried. The Lord do so to me, and more also, If anything but death parts you and me."

A.	Ruth	C.	Naomi
B.	Esther	D.	Peninnah

5. "Let her glean even among the sheaves, and do not reproach her. Also let grain from the bundles fall purposely for her; leave it that she may glean, and do not rebuke her."

A.	Boaz	C.	Perez
B.	David	D.	Jesse

WHO SAID THAT?
OLD TESTAMENT – SHEET #10

Read each statement then identify the speaker by circling A, B, C, or D. Statements are taken from Old and New Testament scriptures.

1. "It is good, my daughter, that you go out with his young women, and that people do not meet you in any other field."

A.	Naomi	C.	Anna
B.	Deborah	D.	Puah

2. "Take Aaron and his sons with him, and the garments, the anointing oil, a bull as the sin offering, two rams, and a basket of unleavened bread; and gather all the congregation together at the door of the tabernacle of meeting."

A.	The Lord	C.	High Priest
B.	The Elders	D.	Joshua

3. 'By those who come near Me I must be regarded as holy; And before all the people I must be glorified.'

A.	Uzziel	C.	The Lord
B.	Michael	D.	Elzaphan

4. "Do not uncover your heads nor tear your clothes, lest you die, and wrath come upon all the people. But let your brethren, the whole house of Israel, bewail the burning which the LORD has kindled. You shall not go out from the door of the tabernacle of meeting, lest you die, for the anointing oil of the LORD is upon you."

A.	Aaron	C.	Eleazar
B.	Moses	D.	Ithamar

5. Two are better than one, Because they have a good reward for their labor. For if they fall, one will lift up his companion. But woe to him who is alone when he falls, For he has no one to help him up."

A.	David	C.	Solomon
B.	Saul	D.	Deborah

WHO SAID THAT?
OLD TESTAMENT – SHEET #11

Read each statement then identify the speaker by circling A, B, C, or D. Statements are taken from Old and New Testament scriptures.

1. You are not able to go against this Philistine to fight with him; for you are a youth, and he a man of war from his youth."

A.	David	C.	Eliab
B.	Saul	D.	Nathan

2. "The LORD, who delivered me from the paw of the lion and from the paw of the bear, He will deliver me from the hand of this Philistine."

A.	David	C.	Jesse
B.	Eliab	D.	Herod

3. "Come to me, and I will give your flesh to the birds of the air and the beasts of the field!"

A.	Goliath the Philistine	C.	Samson
B.	Samuel	D.	Pilate

4. "Abner, whose son is this youth?"

A.	Saul	C.	Jonathan
B.	Peter	D.	Samson

5. "Whose son are you, young man?"

A.	Saul	C.	Abner
B.	David	D.	Samuel

WHO SAID THAT?
NEW TESTAMENT – SHEET #12

Read each statement then identify the speaker by circling A, B, C, or D. Statements are taken from Old and New Testament scriptures.

1. "Are You the King of the Jews?"

A.	Barabbas	C.	Centurion
B.	Caiphas	D.	Pilate

2. "Whom do you want me to release to you? Barabbas, or Jesus who is called Christ?"

A.	Pilate	C.	Caiphas
B.	Cornelius	D.	Zairus

3. "Do not be afraid, for I know that you seek Jesus who was crucified. He is not here; for He is risen, as He said. Come, see the place where the Lord lay."

A.	Moses	C.	Angel
B.	Aaron	D.	Elijah

4. "You are My beloved Son, in whom I am well pleased."

A.	Jesus	C.	Zebedee
B.	Joseph	D.	God

5. "Follow Me, and I will make you become fishers of men."

A.	God	C.	Herod
B.	John	D.	Jesus

WHO SAID THAT?
NEW TESTAMENT – SHEET #13

Read each statement then identify the speaker by circling A, B, C, or D. Statements are taken from Old and New Testament scriptures.

1. "Let us alone! What have we to do with You, Jesus of Nazareth? Did You come to destroy us? I know who You are—the Holy One of God!"

A.	Man with Unclean Spirit	C.	Leper
B.	Mary Magdalene	D.	Herod Agrippa

2. "Be quiet and come out of him!"

A.	God	C.	Jesus
B.	Peter	D.	Roman Centurion

3. "If You are willing, You can make me clean."

A.	Salome	C.	Sanhedrin
B.	Leper	D.	Judas Iscariot

4. "I am willing; be cleansed."

A.	Gabriel	C.	Jesus
B.	God	D.	Moses

5. "Why does this Man speak blasphemies like this? Who can forgive sins but God alone?"

A.	Scribes	C.	Pharisees
B.	Sadducees	D.	Disciples

WHO SAID THAT?

NEW TESTAMENT – SHEET #14

Read each statement then identify the speaker by circling A, B, C, or D. Statements are taken from Old and New Testament scriptures.

1. "Assuredly, I say to you, all sins will be forgiven the sons of men, and whatever blasphemies they may utter; but he who blasphemes against the Holy Spirit never has forgiveness, but is subject to eternal condemnation" — because they said, "He has an unclean spirit."

A.	God	C.	Mary
B.	Jesus	D.	Martha

2. "If only I may touch His clothes, I shall be made well."

A.	Elizabeth	C.	Herodias
B.	Mary	D.	Hemorrhaging Woman

3. "Daughter, your faith has made you well. Go in peace, and be healed of your affliction."

A.	Job	C.	Jacob
B.	Jesus	D.	John

4. "A prophet is not without honor except in his own country, among his own relatives, and in his own house."

A.	God	C.	Jeremiah
B.	Moses	D.	Jesus

5. "Men of Galilee, why do you stand gazing up into heaven? This same Jesus, who was taken up from you into heaven, will so come in like manner as you saw Him go into heaven."

A.	Peter	C.	Two Men in White Apparel
B.	Paul	D.	Abraham

WHO SAID THAT?
NEW TESTAMENT – SHEET #15
Read each statement then identify the speaker by circling A, B, C, or D. Statements are taken from Old and New Testament scriptures.

1. "Men of Judea and all who dwell in Jerusalem, let this be known to you, and heed my words. For these are not drunk, as you suppose, since it is *only* the third hour of the day."

A.	Paul	C.	Peter
B.	Matthew	D.	James

2. "Repent, and let every one of you be baptized in the name of Jesus Christ for the remission of sins; and you shall receive the gift of the Holy Spirit. For the promise is to you and to your children, and to all who are afar off, as many as the Lord our God will call."

A.	Peter	C.	Andrew
B.	Philip	D.	Jude

3. "Silver and gold I do not have, but what I do have I give you: In the name of Jesus Christ of Nazareth, rise up and walk."

A.	John	C.	Peter
B.	Bartholomew	D.	Thaddeus

4. "And now I say to you, keep away from these men and let them alone; for if this plan or this work is of men, it will come to nothing; but if it is of God, you cannot overthrow it—lest you even be found to fight against God."

A.	Peter	C.	Philip
B.	Paul	D.	Thomas

5. "Take your sandals off your feet, for the place where you stand is holy ground.

A.	Peter	C.	The Lord
B.	Nicodemus	D.	Sadducees

WHO SAID THAT?
NEW TESTAMENT – SHEET #16

Read each statement then identify the speaker by circling A, B, C, or D. Statements are taken from Old and New Testament scriptures.

1. "Lord Jesus, receive my spirit."

A.	Peter	C.	Judas
B.	Stephen	D.	Barnabus

2. "Lord, do not charge them with this sin."

A.	Centurion	C.	Stephen
B.	Pharisee	D.	John the Baptist

3. "Lord, I have heard from many about this man, how much harm he has done to Your saints in Jerusalem. And here he has authority from the chief priests to bind all who call on Your name."

A.	Peter	C.	Saul
B.	James	D.	Ananias

4. "Go, for he is a chosen vessel of Mine to bear My name before Gentiles, kings, and the children of Israel. For I will show him how many things he must suffer for My name's sake."

A.	The Lord	C.	Phinehas
B.	Cleophas	D.	Lucifer

5. For you were once darkness, but now *you are* light in the Lord. Walk as children of light (for the fruit of the Spirit is in all goodness, righteousness, and truth), finding out what is acceptable to the Lord."

A.	Peter	C.	Paul
B.	David	D.	James

WHO SAID THAT?
NEW TESTAMENT – SHEET #17

Read each statement then identify the speaker by circling A, B, C, or D. Statements are taken from Old and New Testament scriptures.

1. "Therefore be imitators of God as dear children. And walk in love, as Christ also has loved us and given Himself for us, an offering and a sacrifice to God for a sweet-smelling aroma."

| A. | Peter | C. | Philip |
| B. | Apostle Paul | D. | Andrew |

2. "Children, obey your parents in the Lord, for this is right. Honor your father and mother, which is the first commandment with promise: that it may be well with you and you may live long on the earth."

| A. | Matthias | C. | Peter |
| B. | Andrew | D. | Apostle Paul |

3. "Be anxious for nothing, but in everything by prayer and supplication, with thanksgiving, let your requests be made known to God;"

| A. | Peter | C. | Timothy |
| B. | Apostle Paul | D. | John |

4. "If you knew the gift of God, and who it is who says to you, 'Give Me a drink,' you would have asked Him, and He would have given you living water."

| A. | God | C. | Angel |
| B. | Jesus | D. | Elijah |

5. "Sir, give me this water, that I may not thirst, nor come here to draw."

| A. | Lydia | C. | Sapphira |
| B. | Dorcas | D. | Samaritan Woman |

WHO SAID THAT?
NEW TESTAMENT – SHEET #18

Read each statement then identify the speaker by circling A, B, C, or D. Statements are taken from Old and New Testament scriptures.

1. "Where shall we buy bread, that these may eat?"

A.	Philip	C.	Andrew
B.	Simon	D.	Jesus

2. "Two hundred denarii worth of bread is not sufficient for them, that every one of them may have a little."

A.	Philip	C.	Peter
B.	John	D.	Paul

3. "There is a lad here who has five barley loaves and two small fish, but what are they among so many?"

A.	Andrew	C.	Philip
B.	Peter	D.	Paul

4. "I am the bread of life. He who comes to Me shall never hunger, and he who believes in Me shall never thirst."

A.	God	C.	Jesus
B.	Holy Spirit	D.	Noah

5. "Lord, give us this bread always."

A.	People Christ Fed	C.	Paul and Barnabus
B.	Paul and Silas	D.	Peter and Andrew

WHO SAID THAT?
NEW TESTAMENT – SHEET #19
Read each statement then identify the speaker by circling A, B, C, or D. Statements are taken from Old and New Testament scriptures.

1. "You are not yet fifty years old, and have You seen Abraham?"

A.	Scribes	C.	Jews
B.	Pharisees	D.	Gentiles

2. "This Man is not from God, because He does not keep the Sabbath."

A.	Pharisees	C.	Sadducees
B.	Scribes	D.	Jews

3. "He is a prophet."

A.	Blind Man	C.	Man by Pool of Bethesda
B.	Hemorrhaging woman	D.	Leper

4. "For a good work we do not stone You, but for blasphemy, and because You, being a Man, make Yourself God."

A.	Jews	C.	Roman Soldiers
B.	Pharisees	D.	Sanhedrin

5. "Lord, if You had been here, my brother would not have died. But even now I know that whatever You ask of God, God will give You."

A.	Mary	C.	Elizabeth
B.	Martha	D.	Salome

WHO SAID THAT?
NEW TESTAMENT – SHEET #20

Read each statement then identify the speaker by circling A, B, C, or D. Statements are taken from Old and New Testament scriptures.

1. "Lord, by this time there is a stench, for he has been dead four days."

A.	Mary	C.	Elizabeth
B.	Martha	D.	Anna

2. "Did I not say to you that if you would believe you would see the glory of God?"

A.	Jesus	C.	Peter
B.	God	D.	Paul

3. "Lazarus, come forth!"

A.	Peter	C.	Jesus
B.	Paul	D.	Moses

4. "Why was this fragrant oil not sold for three hundred denarii and given to the poor?"

A.	Judas	C.	Jude
B.	Thomas	D.	Bartholomew

5. "Let her alone; she has kept this for the day of My burial. For the poor you have with you always, but Me you do not have always."

A.	Jesus	C.	Peter
B.	God	D.	Paul

WHO SAID THAT?
NEW TESTAMENT – SHEET #21

Read each statement then identify the speaker by circling A, B, C, or D. Statements are taken from Old and New Testament scriptures.

1. "I have both glorified it and will glorify it again."

A.	God	C.	David
B.	Angel	D.	Moses

2. "And I, if I am lifted up from the earth, will draw all peoples to Myself."

A.	God	C.	Enoch
B.	Jesus	D.	Elijah

3. "A little while longer the light is with you. Walk while you have the light, lest darkness overtake you; he who walks in darkness does not know where he is going. While you have the light, believe in the light, that you may become sons of light."

A.	God	C.	Jesus
B.	Abraham	D.	Jacob

4. "Lord, why can I not follow You now? I will lay down my life for Your sake."

A.	Peter	C.	John
B.	Paul	D.	Philip

5. "Lord, we do not know where You are going, and how can we know the way?"

A.	Andrew	C.	John
B.	Thomas	D.	Matthias

WHO SAID THAT?
NEW TESTAMENT – SHEET #22

Read each statement then identify the speaker by circling A, B, C, or D. Statements are taken from Old and New Testament scriptures.

1. Assuredly, I say to you, today you will be with Me in paradise.

A.	Gabriel	C.	Michael
B.	God	D.	Jesus

2. Rejoice in the Lord always. Again, I will say, rejoice!

A.	Apostle Paul	C.	John
B.	Peter	D.	Luke

3. "This man is the great power of God."

A.	The People of Samaria	C.	Chief Priests
B.	The Blind Man	D.	The People of Philistia

4. "Heaven is My throne, And earth is My footstool. What house will you build for Me?

A.	The Lord	C.	Michael
B.	Gabriel	D.	Satan

5. "Give me this power also, that anyone on whom I lay hands may receive the Holy Spirit."

A.	Simon	C.	Candace
B.	Peter	D.	Philip

WHO SAID THAT?
NEW TESTAMENT – SHEET #23

Read each statement then identify the speaker by circling A, B, C, or D. Statements are taken from Old and New Testament scriptures.

1. "This is My commandment, that you love one another as I have loved you."

A.	Pilate	C.	Caiphas
B.	God	D.	Jesus

2. "If he proves himself a worthy man, not one hair of him shall fall to the earth; but if wickedness is found in him, he shall die."

A.	King Josiah	C.	King David
B.	King Hezekiah	D.	King Solomon

3. The Lord said to my Lord, "Sit at My right hand, till I make Your enemies your footstool."

A.	Jesus	C.	Ahaz
B.	David	D.	Isaiah

4. "Repent and let everyone of you be baptized in the name of Jesus Christ for the remission of sins; and you shall receive the gift of the Holy Spirit."

A.	John the Baptist	C.	Paul
B.	John the Apostle	D.	Peter

5. "Saul, Saul, why are you persecuting Me?"

A.	Jesus of Nazareth	C.	Stephen
B.	Ananias	D.	A Pharisee

WHO SAID THAT?
NEW TESTAMENT – SHEET #24

Read each statement then identify the speaker by circling A, B, C, or D. Statements are taken from Old and New Testament scriptures.

1. "He who believes and is baptized will be saved; but he who does not believe will be condemned."

A.	Peter	C.	Jesus
B.	Stephen	D.	Eunuch

2. "Aeneas, Jesus the Christ heals you arise and make your bed."

A.	Peter	C.	Judas
B.	Saul	D.	Felix

3. "Go, stand in the temple and speak to the people all the words of this life."

A.	The Elders	C.	Gamaliel
B.	The Scribes	D.	An Angel of the Lord

4. "Tabitha, arise."

A.	Jesus	C.	Peter
B.	God	D.	Paul

5. "Cornelius!"

A.	Jesus	C.	An Angel of God
B.	God	D.	Andrew

WHO SAID THAT?
NEW TESTAMENT – SHEET #25

Read each statement then identify the speaker by circling A, B, C, or D. Statements are taken from Old and New Testament scriptures.

1. "Let not your heart be troubled; you believe in God, believe also in Me."

A.	Jesus	C.	Abraham
B.	God	D.	Isaac

2. "I am the true vine, and My Father is the vinedresser."

A.	Uriah	C.	God
B.	Sceva	D.	Jesus

3. "Woman, why are you weeping?"

A.	Pilate	C.	Jesus
B.	Centurion	D.	Two Angels

4. "Because they have taken away my Lord, and I do not know where they have laid Him."

A.	Mary	C.	Mary Magdalene
B.	Martha	D.	Elizabeth

5. "Unless I see in His hands the print of the nails and put my finger into the print of the nails, and put my hand into His side, I will not believe."

A.	Andrew	C.	Thomas
B.	Nathanael	D.	Philip

WHO SAID THAT?
NEW TESTAMENT – SHEET #26

Read each statement then identify the speaker by circling A, B, C, or D. Statements are taken from Old and New Testament scriptures.

1. "Sirs, what must I do to be saved?"

A.	Keeper of the Prison	C.	Zairus
B.	Herod	D.	Pharoah

2. "Believe on the Lord Jesus Christ, and you will be saved, you and your household."

A.	Paul and Silas	C.	Titus
B.	Paul and Timothy	D.	Paul and Barnabas

3. "The sickness is not unto death, but for the glory of God, that the Son of God may be glorified through it."

A.	John	C.	Thomas
B.	Peter	D.	Jesus

4. "I know that he will rise again in the resurrection at the last day."

A.	Mary	C.	Michal
B.	Martha	D.	Milcah

5. "I have come as a light into the world, that whoever believes in the should not abide I darkness."

A.	God	C.	Jesus
B.	Mose	D.	Elijah

WHO SAID THAT?
NEW TESTAMENT – SHEET #27

Read each statement then identify the speaker by circling A, B, C, or D. Statements are taken from Old and New Testament scriptures.

1. "Hail, King of the Jews!"

A.	Pilate	C.	Soldiers
B.	Caiphas	D.	Pharisees

2. "Behold, I am bringing Him out to you, that you may know that I find no fault in Him."

A.	Jews	C.	Pharisees
B.	Pilate	D.	Elders

3. "If you let this Man go, you are not Caesar's friend. Whoever makes himself a king speaks against Caesar."

A.	Jews	C.	Greeks
B.	Romans	D.	Pilate

4. "Shall I crucify your King?"

A.	Pilate	C.	Caesar
B.	Caiphas	D.	Herod

5. "I thirst!"

A.	Philip	C.	Paul
B.	John	D.	Jesus

FILL IN THE BLANKS

FILL IN THE BLANKS – SHEET #1

Fill in the appropriate text to complete each NKJV scripture verse.

1. "Let not your _____ be troubled; you believe in_____,

believe also in Me. In My Father's _____ are many_____; if

it were not so, I would have told you. I go to _____a place for you.

2. Jesus said to him, "I am the_____, the_____,

and the _____. No one comes to the_____except

through _____.

3. "If you love Me, keep My _____.

4. And I will _____the Father, and He will give you

another _____, that He may _____with you_____.

5. As the _____loved Me, I also have loved you; _____ in My
love.

FILL IN THE BLANKS – SHEET #2

Fill in the appropriate text to complete each NKJV scripture verse.

1. For the _____ is _____, He loves _____; His

countenance beholds the _____.

2. Beloved, I beg you as _____ and _____,

abstain from fleshly _____ which war against the _____,

3. who Himself bore our _____ in His own _____ on the tree, that

we, having died to _____, might live for

_____by whose _____you were healed.

4. For you were like _____ going _____, but have now returned to

the _____ and _____ of your souls.

5. "Behold, I lay in _____ A chief _____, elect,

_____, And he who _____ on Him will by no

means be put to _____."

FILL IN THE BLANKS – SHEET #3

Fill in the appropriate text to complete each NKJV scripture verse.

1. And of His _____- we have all received, and _____ for grace.

2. Now this is the _____ of John, when the _____ sent priests

and Levites from _____ to ask him, "Who are you?"

3. "Most _____, I say to you, unless one is

_____again, he cannot see the _____ of God."

4. "Most _____, I say to you, unless one is born of _____

and the _____, he cannot enter the _____ of God."

5. If I have told you _____ things and you do not_____,

how will you _____ if I tell you _____ things?

FILL IN THE BLANKS – SHEET #4

Fill in the appropriate text to complete each NKJV scripture verse.

1. He who does not _____ does not know God, for God is_____.

2. In this the love of _____ was manifested toward us, that

_____ has sent His only begotten _____ into the world, that we might

_____ through Him.

3. In this is _____, not that we loved _____, but that He

_____us and sent His _____ *to be* the propitiation for our

_____.

4. Beloved, if _____ so _____ us, we also ought to _____ one

_____.

5. Whoever _____ that _____ is the _____ of

_____, God _____ in him, and he in _____.

FILL IN THE BLANKS – SHEET #5

Fill in the appropriate text to complete each NKJV scripture verse.

1. And we have _____ and _____ the _____

that God has for us. God is _____, and he who _____ in love

_____ in _____, and God in him.

2. And this _____ we have from

_____: that he who loves_____ must _____

his _____ also.

3. "Behold, the _____ shall be with _____, and bare a

_____, and they shall call His name _____," which is translated,

"_____ with _____."

4. "_____, for the _____of _____is at

hand!"

5. And suddenly a _____ came from _____, saying, "This

is My beloved _____, in whom I am well _____."

FILL IN THE BLANKS – SHEET #6

Fill in the appropriate text to complete each NKJV scripture verse.

1. Man shall not _____by _____ alone, but by every _____

that _____ from the _____ of _____.

2. You shall _____ the _____ your God, and _____

only you shall _____.

3. Follow _____, and I will make you _____ of _____.

4. Blessed are the _____ in _____, For theirs is the _____

of _____.

5. Blessed are those who _____, For they shall be _____.

FILL IN THE BLANKS – SHEET #7

Fill in the appropriate text to complete each NKJV scripture verse.

1. You are the _____ of the _____; but if the _____
loses its _____, how shall it be _____? It is then
_____ for nothing but to be _____ out and _____ underfoot
by men.

2. You are the _____ of the _____. A _____ that
is set on a _____ cannot be _____.

3. Do not think that I came to _____ the _____ or the
_____. I did not come to _____ but to _____.

4. For if you _____ men their _____, your heavenly _____
will also _____ you.

5. No one can _____ two _____; for either he will _____
the one and _____ the other, or else he will be _____ to the
one and _____ the other.

FILL IN THE BLANKS – SHEET #8

Fill in the appropriate text to complete each NKJV scripture verse.

1. _____, and let every one of you be _____ in the name

of _____ _____ for the _____ of

sins; and you shall receive the _____ of the _____ _____.

2. Sing to the _____ a new _____, And His _____ in the

_____ of saints.

3. Trust in the _____ with all your _____, And _____ not on

your own _____;

4. In all your ways _____ Him, And He shall _____your paths.

5. Happy is the _____ who finds _____, And the _____ who gains

_____;

FILL IN THE BLANKS – SHEET #9

Fill in the appropriate text to complete each NKJV scripture verse.

1. For You have made him a little _____ than the _____,

And You have _____ him with _____ and

_____.

2. You have made _____ to have _____ over the works of Your

_____; You have put all _____ under his _____,

3. For the _____ *is* _____, He loves _____;

His countenance beholds the _____.

4. I will sing to the _____, Because He has dealt _____

with me.

5. In my _____ I _____ to the _____,

And He _____ me.

143

FILL IN THE BLANKS – SHEET #10

Fill in the appropriate text to complete each NKJV scripture verse.

1. I will _____ _____ my eyes to the _____— From whence

_____ my help? My help _____ from the _____,

Who made _____ and _____.

2. I was _____ when _____ said to me, "Let us _____

into the _____ of the _____."

3. If it had not been the _____ who was on our _____,

4. Blessed is _____ who _____ the LORD, Who_____

in His _____.

5. Behold, how _____ and how _____ it is

For _____to dwell _____ in _____!

FILL IN THE BLANKS – SHEET #11

Fill in the appropriate text to complete each NKJV scripture verse.

1. "Then _____ will call on me, but I will not answer; They will _____ me diligently, but they will not _____ me."

2. Because they hated _____ And did not choose the _____ of the LORD,

3. They would have none of my _____And _____ my every rebuke.

4. Therefore they shall eat the _____of their own way And be _____ to the full with their own _____.

5. For the turning away of the _____ will slay them, And the _____of fools will _____ them;

145

FILL IN THE BLANKS – SHEET #12

Fill in the appropriate text to complete each NKJV scripture verse.

1. Praise God in His_____; Praise Him in His mighty_____!

2. Praise Him for His mighty _____; Praise Him according to His

excellent _____!

3. Praise Him with the sound of the_____! Praise Him

with the _____and _____!

4. Praise Him with the _____and _____;

Praise Him with _____ instruments and _____!

5. Praise Him with loud _____; Praise Him with clashing _____!

FILL IN THE BLANKS – SHEET #13

Fill in the appropriate text to complete each NKJV scripture verse.

1. Sing to the LORD a new _____, And His _____ in the

assembly of _____.

2. Let _____ rejoice in their Maker; Let the children of _____

be joyful in their King.

3. Let them _____ His name with the _____; Let them sing

_____ to Him with the _____and

_____.

4. For the LORD takes _____in His _____; He

will _____ the _____with salvation.

5. Let the saints be _____ in glory; Let them _____

aloud on their beds.

FILL IN THE BLANKS – SHEET #14

Fill in the appropriate text to complete each NKJV scripture verse.

1. Make a joyful _____ to the LORD, all you _____!

2. Serve the LORD with _____.

3. Know that the LORD, He is _____; It is He who has _____ us, and not

we _____; We are His _____ and the _____ of

His pasture.

4. Enter into His _____ with _____, And into His courts

with _____.

5. For the LORD is _____; His _____ is everlasting, And His

_____endures to all _____.

FILL IN THE BLANKS – SHEET #15

Fill in the appropriate text to complete each NKJV scripture verse.

1. O LORD, God of my _____, I have _____ out day and night before You.

2. Let my _____ come before You; _____Your ear to my cry.

3. For my _____ is full of _____, And my _____ draws near to the grave.

4. I am counted with those who go _____to the pit; I am like a _____who has no strength,

5. Adrift among the _____, Like the slain who lie in the _____, Whom You _____ no more, And who are cut off from Your _____.

SCRIPTURE CRYPTOGRAMS

SCRIPTURE CRYPTOGRAMS – SHEET #1

To decipher cryptograms, you must substitute one letter for another. Each cryptogram was configured individually. Letters used for one will not solve another. Try to solve the short words first. Pay attention to words with double letters. Try to think of word(s) that make the most sense. The first one has been done for you. Good luck! Have fun!

1. JLLS KYS HCZTJFW TB WFD QLZS.

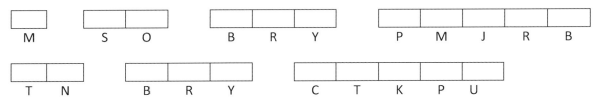

G	O	O	D
J	L	L	S

A	N	D
K	Y	S

U	P	R	I	G	H	T
H	C	Z	T	J	F	W

I	S
T	B

T	H	E
W	F	D

L	O	R	D
Q	L	Z	S

2. M SO BRY PMJRB TN BRY CTKPU.

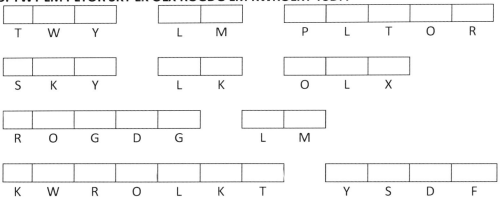

M

S O

B R Y

P M J R B

T N

B R Y

C T K P U

3. TWY LM PLTOR SKY LK OLX ROGDG LM KWROLKT YSDF.

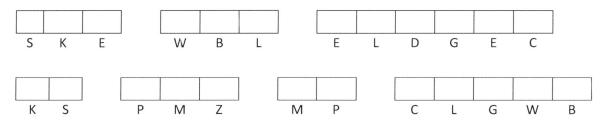

T W Y

L M

P L T O R

S K Y

L K

O L X

R O G D G

L M

K W R O L K T

Y S D F

4. SKE WBL ELDGEC KS PMZ MP CLGWB.

S K E

W B L

E L D G E C

K S

P M Z

M P

C L G W B

SCRIPTURE CRYPTOGRAMS – SHEET #2

5. TKS PCF IK DF LFCNFVI FYFE PG TKSC NPIXFC ME XFPYFE MG LFCNFV.

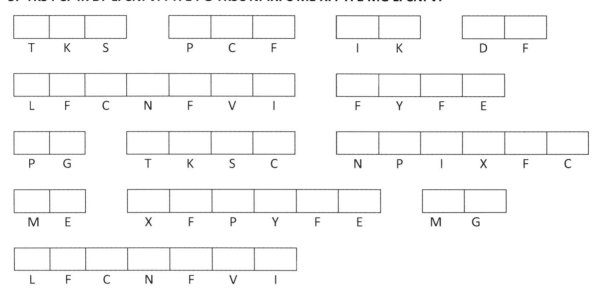

6. SFY BSS KPW CP IF CPTF ZMYG SPZF.

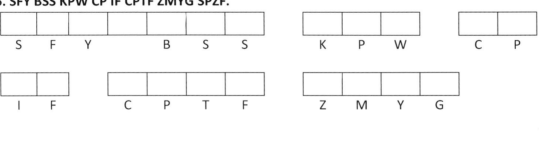

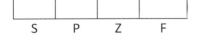

7. CET VF VLPM DN CLGXY, WEX DN HGZYX.

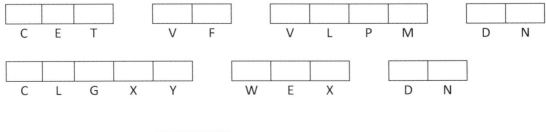

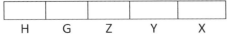

SCRIPTURE CRYPTOGRAMS – SHEET #3

8. WNE TPMSS XNB BYWZB BPY SNGH WNEG DNH.

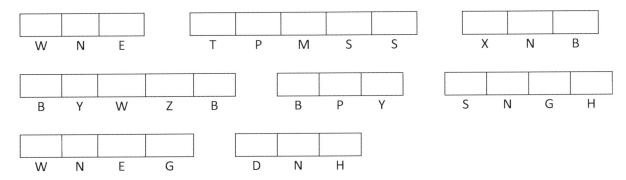

9. SALABF CHS FTA YUBZGHD HC TAWNAB UK WF TWBG.

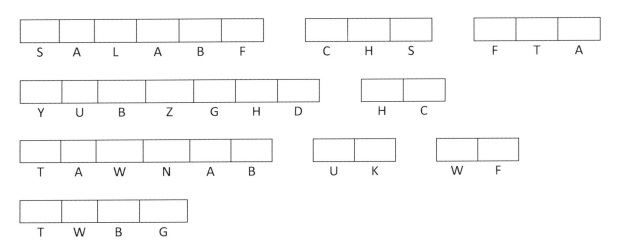

10. STLMT XT PRCB IMN.

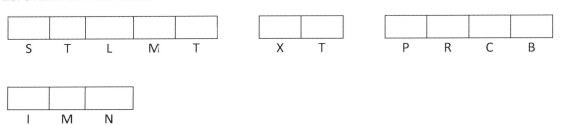

SCRIPTURE CRYPTOGRAMS – SHEET #4

11. KZW BCG DK FZNG Z TZCM HZM.

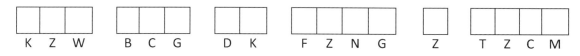

12. ZT KMSC BTDPFY XPBZ BTC GZER LZE TC MY KZZR!

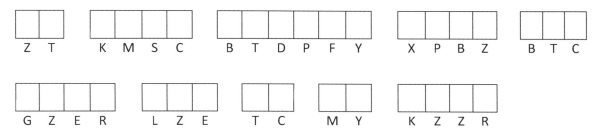

13. K PSPT K, YB FJP CDEG, YTG HPWKGPW BP FJPEP KW TD WYSKDE.

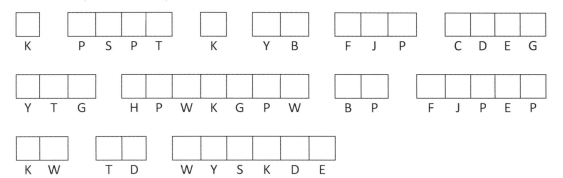

SCRIPTURE CRYPTOGRAMS – SHEET #5

14. P KS BCH WRLJ ZRVL CRWZ RDH, BCH TLHKBRL RI PNLKHW ZRVL MPDO.

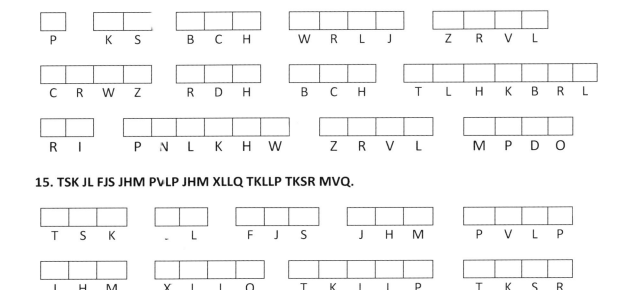

15. TSK JL FJS JHM PVLP JHM XLLQ TKLLP TKSR MVQ.

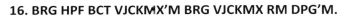

16. BRG HPF BCT VJCKMX'M BRG VJCKMX RM DPG'M.

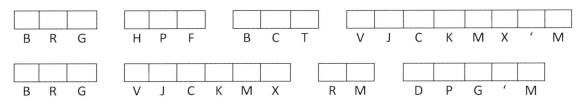

17. SCW BKTS TCFPP POHW DZ UFOSC.

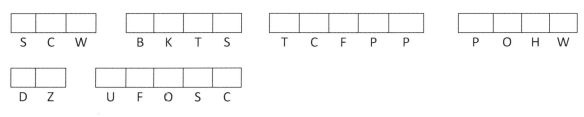

SCRIPTURE CRYPTOGRAMS – SHEET #6

18. O PE WCY ZBSV PGV WCYSY OJGB BWCYS;

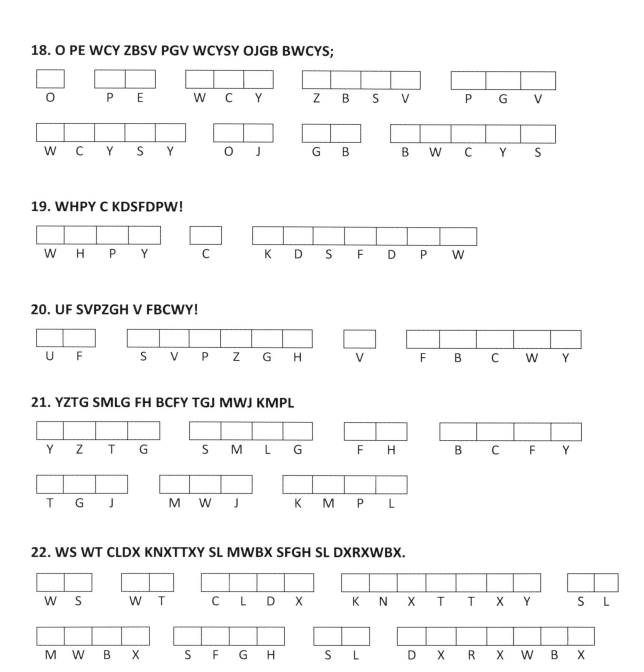

19. WHPY C KDSFDPW!

20. UF SVPZGH V FBCWY!

21. YZTG SMLG FH BCFY TGJ MWJ KMPL

22. WS WT CLDX KNXTTXY SL MWBX SFGH SL DXRXWBX.

SCRIPTURE CRYPTOGRAMS – SHEET #7

23. KMLLSW PMNB CHP WM WVJ GMBU,

K	M	L	L	S	W

P	M	N	B

C	H	P

W	M

W	V	J

G	M	B	U

24. BYTM EQ MJY PLBZ SQZ OSEM KSMEYQMPR CLB JEX

B	Y	T	M

E	Q

M	J	Y

P	L	B	Z

S	Q	Z

O	S	E	M

K	S	M	E	Y	Q	M	P	R

C	L	B

J	E	X

25. GDVJD HTKS VBYDT VBP HKTJVRD FTVXC;

G	D	V	J	D

H	T	K	S

V	B	Y	D	T

V	B	P

H	K	T	J	V	R	D

F	T	V	X	C

26. YSTEY JL YDK PCSN ZLN NC WCCN;

Y	S	T	E	Y

J	L

Y	D	K

P	C	S	N

Z	L	N

N	C

W	C	C	N

27. KRLTML HRQCLPPLP TRPL NY;

K	R	L	T	M	L

H	R	Q	C	L	P	P	L	P

T	R	P	L

N	Y

28. KVRTTRF HT PR ZPMTR JBLSTXBRTTHMS HT DMBXHQRS,

K	V	R	T	T	R	F

H	T

P	R

Z	P	M	T	R

J	B	L	S	T	X	B	R	T	T	H	M	S

H	T

D	M	B	X	H	Q	R	S

29. RTGK ZFSSFNZ ZUTPP LY CF CUY NMDBYX;

R	T	G	K

Z	F	S	S	F	N	Z

Z	U	T	P	P

L	Y

C	F

C	U	Y

N	M	D	B	Y	X

30. HR BW JBBP TBQSYJR

H	R

B	W

J	B	B	P

T	B	Q	S	Y	J	R

SCRIPTURE CRYPTOGRAMS – SHEET #9

31. SKC DGFVC GK SKC ZGMQ FT GDCM SKC YVSCMT;

S	K	C			D	G	F	V	C		G	K		S	K	C		Z	G	M	Q

F	T		G	D	C	M		S	K	C		Y	V	S	C	M	T

32. FTBKP YL PDB NWTJ KMJ FTBKPNV PW CB XTKYLBJ

F	T	B	K	P		Y	L		P	D	B		N	W	T	J		K	M	J

F	T	B	K	P	N	V		P	W		C	B		X	T	K	Y	L	B	J

33. LGR MUKLWP GBUM CSU WXCKGWP

L	G	R		M	U	K	L	W	P		G	B	U	M		C	S	U

W	X	C	K	G	W	P

34. CW JDRB YWGMPX YC YWB SCTV!

C	W		J	D	R	B		Y	W	G	M	P	X

Y	C		Y	W	B		S	C	T	V

SCRIPTURE CRYPTOGRAMS – SHEET #10

35. TS JTR KPXC N ZPY JPDD HNDD PMYR PY

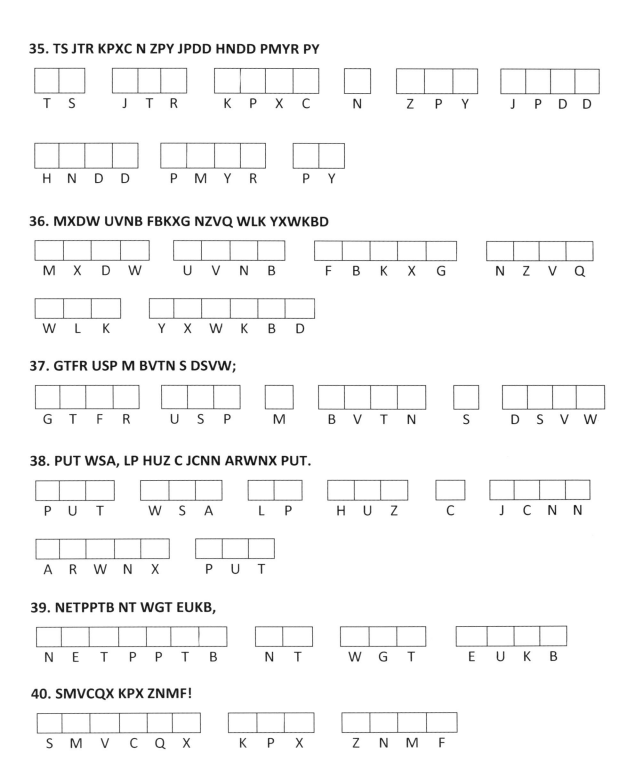

36. MXDW UVNB FBKXG NZVQ WLK YXWKBD

37. GTFR USP M BVTN S DSVW;

38. PUT WSA, LP HUZ C JCNN ARWNX PUT.

39. NETPPTB NT WGT EUKB,

40. SMVCQX KPX ZNMF!

"STATON" THE FACTS
THE INFORMATIVE BIBLE BASED ACTIVITY BOOK

ANSWER SHEETS

ANSWERS TO WORD SCRAMBLES

Sheet #1: 1. Noah, 2. Animals, 3. Flood, 4. Water, 5. Rain, 6. Dove, 7. Raven, 8. Lambs, 9. Elephants, 10. Lions, 11. Giraffes, 12. Obedient, 13. Build, 14. Forty, 15. Family

Sheet #2: 1. Mary, 2. Joseph, 3. Jesus, 4. Wisemen, 5. Shepherd, 6. Manger, 7. Bethlehem, 8. Magi, 9. Gifts, 10. Virgin, 11. Birth, 12. Star, 13. Hope, 14. Joy, 15. Peace

Sheet #3: 1. Eliphaz, 2. Zophar, 3. Bildad, 4. Perfect, 5. Faithful, 6. Suffer, 7. Righteous, 8. Satan, 9. Friends, 10. Repent, 11. Jehovah, 12. Wealthy, 13. Loyal, 14. Trust, 15. Temptation

Sheet #4: 1. Wedding, 2. Water, 3. Mary, 4. Jesus, 5. Wine, 6. Waterpots, 7. Bride, 8. Groom, 9. Best, 10. Good, 11. Galilee, 12. Food, 13. Grapes, 14. Mother, 15. Disciples

Sheet #5: 1. Daniel, 2. Deliverance, 3. Ninety, 4. Lions, 5. Powerful, 6. Captivity, 7. Honor, 8. Empire, 9. God, 10. Den, 11. Brave, 12. Strong, 13. Protect, 14. Safe, 15. Defeat

Sheet #6: 1. Grace, 2. Abound, 3. Love, 4. Mercy, 5. Blessing, 6. Israel, 7. Repent, 8. Messiah, 9. Forgive, 10. Heal, 11. Backsliders, 12. Sufficient, 13. Almighty, 14. Favor, 15. Goodness

Sheet #7: 1. Giant, 2. Shepherd, 3. Slingshot, 4. Stone, 5. David, 6. Goliath, 7. Brave, 8. Champion, 9. Combat, 10. Philistine, 11. Tall, 12. Mighty, 13. Saul, 14. King, 15. Warrior

Sheet 8: 1. Judgment, 2. Glory, 3. God, 4. Zion, 5. Christ, 6. Deliver, 7. Blessing, 8. Restore, 9. Kingdom, 10. Everlasting, 11, Sovereign, 12. Cloud, 13. Heaven, 14. New Jerusalem

Sheet #9: 1. Branch, 2. Jesus, 3. Savior, 4. Lord, 5. Counselor, 6. Teacher, 7. Prophet, 8. Judge, 9. Word, 10. Redeemer, 11. Messiah, 12. True Vine, 13. Dayspring, 14. Advocate, 15. Lamb

Sheet #10: 1. Jehovah, 2. Wonderful, 3. Shiloh, 4. Son, 5. Nazarene, 6. Morning Star, 7. Prince of Peace, 8. Root of David, 9. King of Kings, 10. Holy One, 11. Alpha and Omega, 12. Bread of Life, 13. Cornerstone, 14. First and Last, 15. Everlasting Father

ANSWERS TO WORD SCRAMBLES

Sheet #11: 1. Shadrach, 2. Meshach, 3. Abednego, 4. Jewish, 5. Three, 6. Men, 7. Daniel, 8. Fire, 9. God, 10. King, 11. Babylon, 12. Samuel, 13. Christ, 14. Sheltered, 15. Untouchable

Sheet #12: 1. Love, 2. Joy, 3. Peace, 4. Patience, 5, Kindness, 6. Goodness, 7. Faithfulness, 8. Gentleness, 9. Meekness, 10. Self-Control, 11. Paul, 12. Epistle, 13. Galatians, 14. Kingdom, 15. Repentance

Sheet #13: 1. Cain, 2. Abel, 3. Seth, 4. Murder, 5. Sin, 6. Fruit, 7. Yahweh, 8. Satan, 9. Garden, 10. Eden, 11. Serpent, 12. Forbidden, 13. Good, 14. Evil, 15. Naked

Sheet#14: 1. Covenant, 2. Promise, 3. Father, 4. Nation, 5. Ishmael, 6. Isaac, 7. Sarah, 8. Abram, 9. Lord, 10. Protect, 11, Hagar, 12. Faith, 13. Descendants, 14. History, 15. Blessing

Sheet #15: 1. Rachel, 2. Leah, 3. Gad, 4. Naphtali, 5. Simeon, 6. Levi, 7. Judah, 8. Asher, 9. Reuben, 10. Benjamin, 11. Joseph, 12. Issachar, 13. Zebulun, 14. Dan, 15. Dinah

Sheet #16: 1. Genesis, 2. Corinthians, 3. Leviticus, 4. Philemon, 5. Deuteronomy, 6. Revelation, 7. Judges, 8. Obadiah, 9. Samuel, 10. Timothy, 11. Chronicles, 12. Proverbs, 13. Nehemiah, 14. Titus, 15. Job

Sheet #17: 1. Exodus, 2. Romans, 3. Numbers, 4. Ephesians, 5. Joshua, 6. Hebrews, 7. Ruth, 8. Jeremiah, 9. Kings, 10. Matthew, 11. Ezra, 12. Zephaniah, 13. Micah, 14. Psalms, 15. Habakkuk

Sheet #18: 1. John, 2. Jonah, 3. Peter, 4. Nahum, 5. Daniel, 6. Haggai, 7. Romans, 8. Colossians, 9. Malachi, 10. Mark, 11. Isaiah, 12. Philippians, 13. Esther, 14. Lamentations, 15. Thessalonians

Sheet #19: 1. Zechariah, 2. Ecclesiastes, 3. Song of Solomon, 4. Jude, 5. Acts, 6. Luke, 7. Joel, 8. Hosea, 9. Amos, 10. James, 11. Ezekiel

Sheet #20: 1. Hosea, 2. Beeri, 3. Uzziah, 4. Jotham, 5. Ahaz, 6. Hezekiah, 7. Gomer, 8. Diblaim, 9. Jezreel, 10. Jehu, 11. Lo-Ruhamah, 12. Lo-Ammi, 13. David, 14. Ephraim, 15. Judah

ANSWERS TO WORD SCRAMBLES

Sheet #21: 1. Tekoa, 2. Carmel, 3. Damascus, 4. Gilead, 5. Hazael, 6. Kir, 7. Gaza, 8. Ashdod, 9. Ashkelon, 10. Tyre, 11. Ekron, 12. Edom, 13. Bozrah, 14. Ammon, 15. Teman

Sheet 22: 1. Jonah, 2. Nineveh, 3. Joppa, 4. Tarshish, 5. Affliction, 6. Billows, 7. Waves, 8. Fish, 9. Cargo, 10. Ship, 11. Land, 12. Belly, 13. Mercy, 14. Prayed, 15. Temple

Sheet #23: 1. Jesus Christ, 2. David, 3. Abraham, 4. Isaac, 5. Jacob, 6. Perez, 7. Zerah, 8. Tamar, 9. Boaz, 10. Nahshon, 11. Obed, 12. Solomon, 13. Ruth, 14. Rehoboam, 15. Abijah

Sheet #24: 1. Nicodemus, 2. Kingdom, 3. Spirit, 4. Destroy, 5. Temple, 6. Passover, 7. Scripture, 8. Build, 9. Womb, 10. Born, 11. Wind, 12. Teacher, 13. Testify, 14. Heavenly, 15. Disciples

Sheet #25: 1. Nations, 2. Rage, 3. Gentiles, 4. Miracle, 5. Holy, 6. Vain, 7. Sadducees, 8. Servant, 9. Companions, 10. Blood, 11. Apostles, 12. Doctrine, 13. Priest, 14. Morning, 15. Children

Sheet #26: 1. Lewdness, 2. Murders, 3. Sorcery, 4. Flesh, 5. Adultery, 6. Fornication, 7. Idolatry, 8. Envy, 9. Wrath, 10. Dearth, 11. Inherit, 12. Neighbor, 13. Faithfulness, 14. Goodness, 15. Kindness

Sheet #27: 1. Lord, 2. Shepherd, 3. Comfort, 4. Valley, 5. Follow, 6. Pastures, 7. Death, 8. Enemies, 9. Forever, 10. Anoint, 11. Righteousness, 12. Goodness, 13. Shadow, 14. Mercy, 15. Staff

Sheet #28: 1. Peter, 2. Herod, 3. Imprison, 4. John, 5. James, 6. Garment, 7. Vision, 8. Sandals, 9. Jewish, 10. Depart, 11. Struck, 12. Victim, 13. Knock, 14. Gate, 15. Girl

Sheet #29: 1. Daughter, 2. Saul, 3. King, 4. Messenger, 5. Younger, 6. Jonathan, 7. David, 8. Whirl, 9. Battle, 10. Death, 11. Dance, 12. Sister, 13. Tonight, 14. Window, 15. Morning

Sheet #30: 1. Sister, 2. Leah, 3. Brother, 4. Defile, 5. Kind, 6. Shechem, 7, Hamor, 8. Hivite, 9. Simeon, 10. Levi, 11. Sword, 12. Wedding, 13. Marry, 14. Union, 15. Bride

ANSWERS TO WORD SCRAMBLES

Sheet #31: 1. Fearless, 2. Faithful, 3. Humble, 4. Wise, 5. Hebrew, 6. Brave, 7. Prophet, 8. Judah, 9. Israel, 10. Clever, 11. Jeroboam, 12. Book, 13. Farmer, 14. Herder, 15. Visions

Sheet #32: 1. Invocation, 2. Prayer, 3. Sermon, 4. Introduction, 5. Closing, 6. Song, 7. Blessing, 8. Offering, 9. Benediction, 10. Worship, 11. Service, 12. Scripture, 13. Reading, 14. Order, 15. Testimony

Sheet #33: 1. Powerful, 2. Emotional, 3. Judgment, 4. Covenant, 5. Prophet, 6. Solomon, 7. Jerusalem, 8. Commission, 9. Kings, 10. Countrymen, 11. Temple, 12. Judah, 13. Babylon, 14. Nation, 15. Spokesman

Sheet #34: 1. Violence, 2. Conflict, 3. Injustice, 4. Invasion, 5. Punish, 6. Wicked, 7. Successful, 8. Believer, 9. Salvation, 10. Strength, 11. Struggle, 12. Trouble, 13. Disgrace, 14. Rejoice, 15. Deliver

Sheet #35: 1. Announcement, 2. Promise, 3. Future, 4. Repentance, 5. Josiah, 6. Divine, 7. Complaint, 8. Principle, 9. Oppression, 10. Gladness, 11. Punish, 12. Judge, 13. People, 14. Religion, 15. Revive

Sheet #36: 1. Feasts, 2. Vows, 3. Wicked, 4. Nineveh, 5. Guilty, 6. Flood, 7. Collapse, 8. Palace, 9. Gate, 10. River, 11. Enemy, 12. Fall, 13. Universe, 14. Punish, 15. Vengeance

Sheet #37: 1. Protect, 2. Bless, 3. Soldiers, 4. Army, 5. Israel, 6. Fortify, 7. Guard, 8. Border, 9. Rule, 10. Lesson, 11. Dedicate, 12. Future, 13. Immoral, 14. Idolatry, 15. Kingdom

Sheet #38: 1. Message, 2. God, 3. Sovereign, 4. Control, 5. History, 6. Prediction, 7. Jesus, 8. Return, 9. Prophet, 10. Sin, 11. Period, 12. Blessing, 13. Savior, 14. Almighty, 15. Lord

Sheet #39: 1. Bethlehem, 2. Little, 3. Thousand, 4. Ruler, 5. Stand, 6. Feed, 7. Flock, 8. Strength, 9. Majesty, 10. Name, 11. Abide, 12. Great, 13. Peace, 15. Prophecy

Sheet #40: 1. Locusts, 2. Swarm, 3. Strip, 4. Vegetation, 5. Vision, 6. Hoard, 7. Devastate, 8. Intervene, 9. Punish, 10. Pity, 11. Generation, 12. Land, 13. Interpret, 14. Sorrow, 15. Plague

ANSWERS TO WORD SCRAMBLES

Sheet #41: 1. True, 2. False, 3. Lie, 4. Announcement, 5. Power, 6. Captive, 7. Noble, 8. Contradiction, 9. Return, 10. Jerusalem, 11. Babylon, 12. Confront, 13. Obey, 14. Listen, 15. Death

Sheet #42: 1. Love, 2. Story, 3. Woman, 4. Christ, 5. Monogamy, 6. Marriage, 7. Friends, 8. Wedding, 9. Song, 10. Relationship, 11. Celebration, 12. Husband, 13. Wife, 14. Commitment, 15. Believe

Sheet #43: 1. Wisdom, 2. Understanding, 3. Instruction, 4. Perception, 5. Judgment, 6. Justice, 7. Guarantee, 8. Guidance, 9. Information, 10. Decision, 11. Concern, 12. Consequence, 13. Knowledge, 14. Morality, 15. Discipline

Sheet #44: 1. Naomi, 2. Kinsman, 3. Union, 4. Inheritance, 5. Marry, 6. Boaz, 7. Estate, 8. Penalty, 9. Faith, 10. Obed, 11. Mother, 12. Support, 13. Daughter, 14. Pleasant, 15. Beauty

Sheet #45: 1. Samson, 2. Passion, 3. Prostitute, 4. Philistines, 5. Moral, 6. Spiritual, 7. Weakness, 8. Judge, 9. Secret, 10. Gifts, 11. Oppression, 12. Deliver, 13. Potential, 14. Incident, 15. Physical

Sheet #46: 1. Government, 2. Monarchy, 3. Nation, 4. Anarchy, 5. Poverty, 6. Wealth, 7. Territory, 8. Political, 9. Worship, 10. Center, 11. World, 12. Hebrew, 13. Descendants, 14. Chosen, 15. Jews

Sheet #47: 1. Canaan, 2. Israelites, 3. Spies, 4. Jericho, 5. Jordan, 6. River, 7. Circumcise, 8. Passover, 9. Victory, 10. Preparation, 11. Challenge, 12. Leader, 13. Promise, 14. Conquest, 15. Division

Sheet #48: 1. Woman, 2. Prophetess, 3. Leader, 4. Judge, 5. Northern, 6. Tribes, 7. Israelite, 8. Forty, 9. Years, 10. Peace, 11. Power, 12. Political, 13. Executive, 14. Legislative, 15. Judicial

Sheet #49: 1. Burnt, 2. Grain, 3. Fellowship, 4. Peace, 5. Sin, 6. Purification, 7. Guilt, 8. Confess, 9. Blood, 10. Atonement, 11. Forgiven, 12. Sacrifice, 13. Offering, 14. Devotion, 15. Thanksgiving

Sheet #50: 1. Honor, 2. Name, 3. Vain, 4. Murder, 5. Mother, 6. Father, 7. Commit, 8. Adultery, 9. Steal, 10. Covet, 11. Testify, 12. Loving, 13. Faithful, 14. Good, 15. Holy

ANSWERS TO WORD MATCHES

Sheet #01: F, C, I, J, H, D, G, E, B, A

Sheet #02: I, F, G, A, H, B, C, E, J, D

Sheet #03: F, D, G, J, A, H, C, I, B, E

Sheet #04: E, F, G, A, I, C, J, B, D, H

Sheet #05: D, E, A, H, G, B, C, F, J, I

Sheet #06: G, J, H, E, B, C, I, D, A, F

Sheet #07: G, A, H, E, C, J, B, D, F, I

Sheet #08: H, J, I, G, B, D, C, F, E, A

Sheet #09: E, G, H, F, I, C, J, D, B, A

Sheet #10: I, F, H, A, B, C, D, E, G, J

Sheet #11: E, G, J, B, I, H, D, C, F, A

Sheet #12: J, H, G, I, A, B, C, E, F, D

Sheet #13: J, G, F, A, H, C, I, D, B, E

Sheet #14: I, J, H, A, B, C, D, F, G, E

Sheet #15: F, D, I, A, H, J, G, B, C, E

Sheet #16: C, F, I, D, J, E, H, B, A, G

Sheet #17: E, I, A, G, H, B, C, J, F, D

Sheet #18: I, G, D, J, C, A, E, B, H, F

Sheet #19: A, D, J, G, C, B, H, E, I, F

Sheet #20: E, J, H, B, C, A, F, D, G, I

Sheet #21: F, J, E, I, A, H, D, C, B, G

Sheet #22: F, C, G, A, H, B, D, E, J, I

Sheet #23: J, I, H, G, A, B, C, E, D, F

Sheet #24: C, F, D, A, H, E, J, I, G, B

Sheet #25: C, I, G, J, E, A, D, F, H, B

Sheet #26: H, E, I, B, F, C, J, G, D, A

Sheet #27: F, H, G, B, J, C, I, A, D, E

ANSWER SHEET – WHO SAID THAT?

ANSWERS AND REFERENCE TEXT

Sheet #1: 1-D, 2-C, 3-D, 4-A, 5-A – Gen. 25:30, Judg. 16:6, Ruth 2:12, I Sam. 16:7, 2 Sam. 22:33

Sheet #2: 1-B, 2-C, 3-A. 4-B, 5-A - 1 Sam. 16:12, 18, Job 14:1, Eccl. 5:18, Judg. 13:13

Sheet #3: 1-C, 2-B, 3-A, 4-B, 5-D – Judg. 13:22, Ex. 3:3, 5, 14, 14:13

Sheet #4: 1-C, 2-C, 3-B, 4-D, 5-C – Josh. 2:4, 7:19, 20, 25, Is. 6:5

Sheet #5: 1-C, 2-B, 3-A, 4-B, 5-C – Is. 6:7, 8, 9:6, 11:6, 11:10

Sheet #6: 1-A, 2-C, 3-A, 4-A, 5-B – Gen. 3:12, 13, 22, 4:9, 9:25

Sheet #7: 1-A, 2-A, 3-A, 4-A, 5-A – Gen. 7:3, 13:14, 14:9, 16:5, 16:11

Sheet #8: 1-A, 2-B, 3-B, 4-C, 5-A – Gen. 18:13, 26, 19:2, 17, 32

Sheet #9: 1-A, 2-B, 3-C, 4-A, 5-A – Prov. 10:30, Is. 1:18-20, Judg. 15:16, Ruth 1:16-17; 2:15-16

Sheet #10: 1-A, 2-A, 3-C, 4-B, 5-C – Ruth 2:22, Lev. 8:2, 10:3, 10:6, Eccl. 4:9-10

Sheet #11: 1-B, 2-A, 3-A, 4-A, 5-A – 1 Sam. 17:33, 37, 44, 55, 58

Sheet #12: 1-D, 2-A, 3-C, 4-D, 5-D – Matt. 17:11, 27:17-18, 28:5-6, Mark 1:11, 17

Sheet #13: 1-A, 2-C, 3-B, 4-C, 5-A – Mark 1:24, 25, 40, 41, 2:7

Sheet #14: 1-B, 2-D, 3-B, 4-D, 5-C – Mark 3:28-30, 5:28, 34, 6:4, Acts 1:11

Sheet #15: 1-C, 2-A, 3-C, 4-A, 5-C – Acts 2:14-15, Acts 2:38-39, 3:6, 5:38-39, 7:33

Sheet #16: 1-B, 2-C, 3-D, 4-A, 5-C – Acts 7:59, 60, Acts 9:13-14, 15-16, Eph. 5:8-10

Sheet #17: 1-B, 2-D, 3-B, 4-B, 5-D – Eph. 5:1-2, 6:1-3, Phil. 4:6, John 4:10, 15

Sheet #18: 1-D, 2-A, 3-A, 4-C, 5-A – John 6:5, 7, 9, 35, 34

Sheet #19: 1-C, 2-A, 3-A, 4-A, 5-B – John 8:57, 9:16, 17, 10:33, 11:21-22

Sheet #20: 1-B, 2-A, 3-C, 4-A, 5-A – John 11:39, 40, 43, 12:4, 7

Sheet: #21: 1-A, 2-B, 3-C, 4-A, 5-B – John 12:28; 12:32, 12:35-36; 13:37; 14:5

Sheet #22: 1-D, 2-A, 3-A, 4-A, 5-A – Luke 23:43; Phil. 4:4; Acts 8:10; 7:49, 8:19

Sheet #23: 1-D, 2-D, 3-A, 4-D, 5-A – John 15:2, 1 Kings 1:52, Ps. 110:1, Acts 2:38, Acts 22:7

Sheet #24: 1-C, 2-A, 3-D, 4-C, 5-C – Mark 16:16, Acts 9:34, 5:20, 9:40, 10:3

Sheet #25: 1-A, 2-D, 3-D, 4-C, 5-C – John 14:1, 15:1, 20:13a, 20:13b, 20:25

Sheet #26: 1-A, 2-A, 3-D, 4-B, 5-C – Acts 16:30, 31, John 11:4, 24, 12:46

Sheet #27: 1-C, 2-B, 3-A, 4-A, 5-D - John 19:3, 4, 12, 19:16, 28

ANSWERS TO FILL IN THE BLANKS

Sheet #1

1. John 14:1-2 - "Let not your **heart** be troubled; you believe in **God**, believe also in Me. In My Father's **house** are many **mansions**; if it were not so, I would have told you. I go to **prepare** a place for you.

2. John 14:6 - Jesus said to him, "I am the **way**, the **truth**, and the **life**. No one comes to the **Father** except through **Me**.

3. John 14:15 - "If you love Me, keep My **commandments**.

4. John 14:16 - And I will **pray** the Father, and He will give you another **Helper**, that He may **abide** with you **forever**—

5. John 15:9-10 - As the **Father** loved Me, I also have loved you; **abide** in My love.

Sheet #2

1. Psalm 11:7 - For the LORD *is* **righteous**, He loves **righteousness**; His countenance beholds the **upright**.

2. 1 Peter 2:11 - Beloved, I beg you as **sojourners** and **pilgrims**, abstain from fleshly **lusts** which war against the **soul**,

3. 1 Peter 2:24 - who Himself bore our **sins** in His own **body** on the tree, that we, having died to **sins**, might live for **righteousness**—by whose **stripes** you were healed.

4. 1Peter 2:25 - For you were like **sheep** going **astray** but have now returned to the **Shepherd** and **Overseer** of your souls.

5. 1 Peter 2:6 - "Behold, I lay in **Zion** A chief **cornerstone**, elect, **precious**, And he who **believes** on Him will by no means be put to **shame**."

Sheet #3

1. John 1:16 - And of His **fullness** we have all received, and **grace** for grace.

2. John 1:19 - Now this is the **testimony** of John, when the **Jews** sent priests and Levites from **Jerusalem** to ask him, "Who are you?"

3. John 3:3 - "Most **assuredly**, I say to you, unless one is **born** again, he cannot see the **kingdom** of God."

4. John 3:5 - "Most assuredly, I say to you, unless one is born of **water** and the **Spirit**, he cannot enter the **kingdom** of God.

5. John 3:12 - If I have told you **earthly** things and you do not **believe**, how will you **believe** if I tell you **heavenly** things?

Sheet #4

1. 1 John 4:8 -He who does not **love** does not know God, for God is **love**.

2. 1 John 4:9 - In this the love of **God** was manifested toward us, that **God** has sent His only begotten **Son** into the world, that we might **live** through Him.

3. 1 John 4:10 - In this is **love**, not that we loved **God**, but that He **loved** us and sent His **Son** to be the propitiation for our **sins**.

4 1 John 4:11 - Beloved, if **God** so **loved** us, we also ought to **love** one **another**.

5. 1 John 4:15 - Whoever **confesses** that **Jesus** is the **Son** of **God**, God **abides** in him, and he in **God**.

ANSWERS TO FILL IN THE BLANKS

Sheet #5
1. 1 John 4:16 - And we have **known** and **believed** the **love** that God has for us. God is **love**, and he who **abides** in love **abides** in **God**, and God in him.
2. 1 John 4:21 - And this **commandment** we have from Him: that he who loves **God** must **love** his **brother** also.
3. Matthew 1:23 - "Behold, the **virgin** shall be with **child**, and bear a **Son**, and they shall call His name **Immanuel**," which is translated, "**God** with **us**."
4. Matthew 3:2 - "**Repent**, for the **kingdom** of **heaven** is at hand!"
5. Matthew 3:17 - And suddenly a **voice** *came* from **heaven,** saying, "This is My beloved **Son**, in whom I am well **pleased**."

Sheet #6
1. Matthew 4:4 – "Man shall not **live** by **bread** alone, but by every **word** that **proceeds** from the **mouth** of **God**."
2. Matthew 4:10 – "You shall **worship** the LORD your God, and **Him** only you shall **serve**."
3. Matthew 4:19 - "Follow **Me**, and I will make you **fishers** of **men**."
4. Matthew 5:3 - "Blessed are the **poor** in **spirit**, For theirs is the **kingdom** of **heaven**."
5. Matthew 5:4 - Blessed are those who **mourn**, For they shall be **comforted**.

Sheet #7
1. Matthew 5:13- "You are the **salt** of the **earth**; but if the **salt** loses its **flavor**, how shall it be **seasoned**? It is then good for nothing but to be **thrown** out and **trampled** underfoot by men.
2. Matthew 5:14 - "You are the **light** of the **world**. A **city** that is set on a **hill** cannot be **hidden**.
3. Matthew 5:17 - "Do not think that I came to **destroy** the **Law** or the **Prophets**. I did not come to **destroy** but to **fulfill**.
4. Matthew 6:14 - "For if you **forgive** men their **trespasses**, your heavenly **Father** will also **forgive** you.
5. Matthew 6:24 - "No one can **serve** two **masters**; for either he will **hate** the one and **love** the other, or else he will be **loya**l to the one and **despise** the other. You cannot serve God and mammon.

Sheet 8
1. Acts 2:38 - **Repent** and let every one of you be **baptized** in the name of **Jesus Christ** for the **remission** of sins; and you shall receive the **gift** of the **Holy Spirit**.
2. Psalm 149:1 - Sing to the LORD a new **song**, And His **praise** in the **assembly** of saints.
3. Proverbs 3:5 - Trust in the LORD with all your **heart**, And **lean** not on your own **understanding**;
4. Proverbs 3:6 - In all your ways **acknowledge** Him, And He shall **direct** your paths.
5. Proverbs 3:13 - Happy is the **man** who finds **wisdom**, And the **man** who gains **understanding**;

Sheet #9
1. Psalm 8:5 - For You have made him a little **lower** than the **angels**, And You have **crowned** him with **glory** and **honor**.
2. Psalm 8:6 - You have made **him** to have **dominion** over the works of Your **hands**; You have put all **things** under his **feet**,
3. Psalm 11:7 - For the LORD *is* **righteous**, He loves **righteousness**; His countenance beholds the **upright**.
4. Psalm 13:6 - I will sing to the LORD, Because He has dealt **bountifully** with me.
5. Psalm 120:1 - In my **distress** I **cried** to the LORD, And He **heard** me.

ANSWERS TO FILL IN THE BLANKS

Sheet #10
1. Psalm 121:1-2 - I will <u>lift up</u> my eyes to the **hills**—From whence **comes** my help? My help **comes** from the Lᴏʀᴅ, Who made **heaven** and **earth**.
2. Psalm 122:1 - I was **glad** when **they** said to me, "Let us **go** into the **house** of the Lᴏʀᴅ."
3. Psalm 124:2 - "If it had not been the Lᴏʀᴅ who was on our **side**,
4. Psalm 128:1 - Blessed is **everyone** who **fears** the Lᴏʀᴅ, Who **walks** in His **ways**.
5. Psalm 133:1 - Behold, how **good** and how **pleasant** it is For **brethren** to dwell **together** in **unity**!

Sheet #11
1. Proverbs 1:28 - "Then **they** will call on me, but I will not answer; They will **seek** me diligently, but they will not **find** me.
2. Proverbs 1:29 - Because they hated <u>knowledge</u> And did not choose the <u>fear</u> of the Lᴏʀᴅ,
3. Proverbs 1:30 - They would have none of my **counsel** And **despised** my every rebuke.
4. Proverbs 1:31- Therefore they shall eat the **fruit** of their own way And be **filled** to the full with their own **fancies**.
5. Proverbs 1:32 - For the turning away of the **simple** will slay them, And the **complacency** of fools will **destroy** them;

Sheet #12
1. Psalm 150:1 - Praise God in His **sanctuary**; Praise Him in His mighty **firmament**!
2. Psalm 150:2 - Praise Him for His mighty **acts**; Praise Him according to His excellent **greatness**!
3. Psalm 150:3 - Praise Him with the sound of the **trumpet**; Praise Him with the **lute** and **harp**!
4. Psalm 150:4 - Praise Him with the **timbrel** and **dance**; Praise Him with **stringed** instruments and <u>flutes</u>!
5. Psalm 150:5 - Praise Him with loud **cymbals**; Praise Him with clashing **cymbals**!

Sheet #13
1. Psalm 149:1 - Sing to the Lᴏʀᴅ a new **song**, And His **praise** in the assembly of **saints**.
2. Psalm 149:2 - Let **Israel** rejoice in their Maker; Let the children of **Zion** be joyful in their King.
3. Psalm 149:3 - Let them **praise** His name with the **dance**; Let them sing **praises** to Him with the **timbrel** and **harp**.
4. Psalm 149:4 – For the Lord takes **pleasure** in His **people**; He will **beautify** the **humble** with salvation.
5. Psalm 149:5 - Let the saints be **joyful** in glory; Let them **sing** aloud on their beds.

Sheet #14
1. Psalm 100:1 - Make a joyful **shout** to the Lᴏʀᴅ, all you <u>lands</u>!
2. Psalm 100:2 - Serve the Lᴏʀᴅ with **gladness**;
3. Psalm 100:3 - Know that the Lᴏʀᴅ, He is **God**; It is He who has **made** us, and not we **ourselves**; We are His **people** and the **sheep** of His pasture.
4. Psalm 100:4 - Enter into His **gates** with **thanksgiving**, And into His courts with <u>praise</u>.
5. Psalm 100:5 - For the Lᴏʀᴅ is **good**; His **mercy** is everlasting, And His **truth** endures to all **generations**.

Sheet #15
1. Psalm 88:1 - O Lᴏʀᴅ, God of my **salvation**, I have **cried** out day and night before You.
2. Psalm 88:2 - Let my **prayer** come before You; **Incline** Your ear to my cry.
3. Psalm 88:3 - For my **soul** is full of troubles, And my life draws near to the grave.
4. Psalm 88:4 – I am counted with those who go **down** to the pit; I am like a **man** who has no strength,
5. Psalm 88:5 - Adrift among the **dead**, Like the slain who lie in the **grave**, Whom You **remember** no more, And who are cut off from Your **hand**.

ANSWERS TO WORD SEARCH

WORD SEARCH – SHEET #1
OLD TESTAMENT

AARON
ABRAHAM
ADAM
ARK
BOOK OF GENESIS
COVENANT
DESCENDANTS
DISOBEDIENCE
ESAU
EVE
EXILE
GARDEN OF EDEN
GREAT FLOOD
ISAAC
ISHMAEL
JACOB
JEWISH
KINGDOM
MIDIAN
MOSES
MOUNT SINAI
PASSOVER
REBEKAH
SABBATH
SARAH
SERPENT
TREE OF KNOWLEDGE
TREE OF LIFE
TOWER OF BABEL

```
B O O K O F G E N E S I S A B
M O U N T S I N A I C D U E F
H G A R D E N O F E D E N S D
I J M A X S O W E R I H D M V
A B R A H A M T U X S Q A R K
R L O J E W I S H P O D Y U O
K I N G D O M A M F B R N H I
W V Q U E N C C O V E N A N T
S A B B A T H F S G D J W I L
E X M L B A R T E K I S A A C
R T U C E B P O S T E Y F P K
P R J M L L S V R I N U K A Z
E S A U B E X I L E C M I S A
N F C G H T I J U O E R D H O
T G O N W L A D A M R D H O T
O S S P S C N Y I Q K I M V R
D A A R O N S R L E A A A E E
G R E A T F L O O D P N E R E
E A V H A S O A H D M E L T O
F H R E B E K A H E F Y S L F
I K J T O W E R O F B A B E L
D E S C E N D A N T S E O T I
R A C H E L C H U R N V P N F
T R E E O F K N O W L E D G E
```

WORD SEARCH – SHEET #2
TWELVE TRIBES AND TWELVE PRINCES

REUBEN
SIMEON
LEVI (Not Numbered)
JUDAH
DAN
NAPHTALI
GAD
ASHER
ISSACHAR
ZEBULUN
JOSEPH (Not Numbered)
BENJAMIN
JACOB (Patriarch)
MANASSEH
EPHRAIM
ELIZUR
SHELUMIEL
NAHSHON
NETHANEEL
ELIAB
ELISHAMA
GAMALIEL
ABIDAN
AHIEZER
ELIASAPH
AHIRA
PAGIEL
TRIBES
PRINCES
TWELVE

```
Z E B U L U N J O K M L E V I
A L E N M D A N P F Q G R W S
H I N D A L P Y B C R A D I S
I Z J E R V H D U J U D A H A
E U A R T X T I M Y F S G O C
Z R M O H W A J R E U B E N H
E X I N A O L H D L E L I S A
R L N E U S I M E O N O J W R
U M B R G A Q R P T A V N O T
P A G I E L G D H I L E A X P
Z E B R A J H S R P K R H U C
J O S E P H U M A N A S S E H
S H A R K I T S I W S Y H L R
P R I N C E S O M G H K O I U
N E C T A R I N E K E L N A W
G A M A L I E L T U R N O B X
N I C K P O L Y C A L E B P G
T R A N S F A P O P U L J R S
I A V U I A B I D A N T A I S
C T P M T R I B E S H D C I T
E Q N O E L I A S A P H O N W
F R A N K E N C E N S E B F E
E L I S H A M A M E L T C A L
M Y R W Q L S T A H I R A L Y
N E T H A N E E L P E O D L E
```

WORD SEARCH – SHEET #3
SACRIFICES AND OFFERINGS

ALTAR
AROMA
ATONEMENT
BLOOD
BUILT
BURNT
CHRIST
COMMITMENT
CONFESS
DEVOTION
FELLOWSHIP
FORGIVEN
GOD
GRAIN
GUILT
ISRAELITES
LIVESTOCK
OFFERINGS
PEACE
PIGEONS
PRIEST
PURIFICATION
SACRIFICES
SIN
SYMBOLIZES
TABERNACLE
TURTLEDOVES
UNCLEANNESS
VIOLATION

```
S A C R I F I C E S M L E V O
Y T L N M O A N P I Q G R W F
M O I P A R P Y B N R N D I F
B N V R R G H D U J O D A H E
O E E I T I T I M I E S L O R
L M S E H V A J T G B F T L I
I E T S A E L A N I O A A S N
Z N O T U N C M E O N D R W G
E T C R G I O R P T A V N O S
S A K I F L N D H A R O M A P
Z E B I A J F S R P B U R N T
J G R E P H E M A T A B W S H
S U A R K I S S N W S Y I L G
P I X N C E S E M G X R N I R
B L O O D R M N E K H L M A A
G T M A L T E L T C R N O B I
N I C K I O V I O L A T I O N
S H E M U P I G E O N S Y C G
T R M N I S R A E L I T E S D
I O V U T U R T L E D O V E S
C T P M G R I K E S P E A C E
L E G I O I V I C T O R Y D F
D E V O T I O N E N S E R F U
U N C L E A N N E S S T C A I
T A B E R N A C L E I R A L L
F E L L O W S H I P E O D X T
```

WORD SEARCH – SHEET #4
1 SAMUEL

ADVERSARY
AFFLICTION
ANOINTED
BEERSHEBA
CHERUBIM
EXALT
ELKANAH
GRIEF
HAIR
HANNAH
HOPNI
KING
MAIDSERVANT
PENINNAH
PHILISTINES
PHINEHAS
PROPHET
RAMAH
RAZOR
SAMUEL
SACRIFICE
SHILOH
VINEYARD
VISION
WICKED
WORSHIPPED

```
E L K A N A H J O K M H A I R
R A M A H D A N P V Q G R W S
H I N D A L P E N I N N A H D
H A N N A H H X U S U D A H S
M U A R T X T A M I E S W O A
A R M O H W A L L A O B F O L M
I X I N A O L T D N E L R S U E
D L A F F L I C T I O N S W E
S H I L O H Q U P T A V H O L
E A G I E O G D H I L E I X P
R E B R A P H S R P K B P U W
V O S E P N U H A N A E P E I
A H A R K I C S I W S X E L C
N R I N C E K I N G H O D I K
T E C T A R I N E K E I M A E
G A M C H E R U B I M C O B D
B E E R S H E B A A L E B P U
S H E L U M I E L N P Q R S G
T R A N S R A Z O R U L A R A
I A V U G R I E F A N T U A N
S A C R I F I C E S Y D F I O
E Q N O E L P H I N E H A S L
P R O P H E T C E N S E R F N
K U J S H A V I N E Y A R D T
P H I L I S T I N E S R A L E
A D V E R S A R Y P E O D U D
```

ANSWERS TO WORD SEARCH

WORD SEARCH – SHEET #5
2 SAMUEL

ABISHAI
ABSALOM
AHIMAAZ
AHITHOPHEL
BATTLE
CAPTAINS
CHARIOTS
CONCUBINES
CONSPIRACY
COUNSELOR
GILONITE
JERUSALEM
JOAB
JONATHAN
KING DAVID
KINGDOM
MEPHIBOSHETH
RAISINS
SERVANT
SAUL
TAMAR
TEREBINTH
WEEPING
WINE
ZERUIAH
ZIBA

```
A B S A L O M J O K M J O A B
A L E N M D A N P I Q E R B S
H I N D A L P Y B N R R D I Z
C A P T A I N S U G U U A S E
E H A F T X T I M D E S G H R U
Z I M K H W A J A A B A E A U I
E M I I A O L H D V E L I I N
R A N N U S I M E I N E J W A H
P Z G D E L G D H I L E A X P
Z E B O A J G I L O N I T E C
J O S M P H U M A N A S S E O U
M E P H I B O S H E T H O L U N
J O N A T H A N M G H K N I S
T E R E B I N T H K E L M A E
G A M A L R A I S I N S O B E
N I C K P O L Y C A L E B P L O
S H E L U M I E L N P Q R S O
C O N C U B I N E S U L A R R
I A V U I A B A T T L E T A S
C T P M T R I B S E R V A N T
S A U L E L I W I N E H M N W
F R A W E E P I N G S E A F Z
C O N S P I R A C Y L T R A I
M Y R W C H A R I O T S A L B
A H I T H O P H E L E O D L A
```

WORD SEARCH – SHEET #6
THE BOOK OF PSALMS

ANOINT
ASSEMBLY
CONGREGATION
DECEITFULLY
EARTH
EVERLASTING
GENERATION
HABITATION
HEART
KING OF GLORY
LIGHT
MERCY
MUSICIAN
PASTURES
POTSHERD
REDEEM
RIGHTEOUSNESS
SACRIFICE
SALVATION
SHADOW
SHEPHERD
STRENGTH
VALLEY
VINDICATE
WAR
WORSHIP

```
M U S I C I A N O K M L E D S
E L T N M D N N P F Q G R E C A L
R I R D R L O Y O C R A I I C E
C Z E E E V I D T J U D G E I T
Y U N R D I N I S Y E S H I T A
Z R G O E N T J H E A R T T O N
A X T N E D L H E L E L E U U
S L H E M I I M R O N O O L
S M B R G C Q R D T A V U L P
E V E R L A S T I N G E S S Y K
M E B R A T H D R P K R N V I
B O S E P E R M A N C S E E N
L H G E N E R A T I O N S E L G
Y R I N H E S O M G N K S I O
N E C P A R I N E K G H M A F
G A E A L I G H T U R A O B F
N H C S P O L Y C A E B B P G L
S H E T U M I E E N G I R A O
T R A U S F A C O P A T A W R
I A V R I A I W A T A W A Y
C T P E T F I B O E I T F I
E Q N S I L I A R A O I K N W
F R A R K E N C S R N O R F E
E L C S H A M A H T L N C A L
S H A D O W E E P V A L L E Y
```

WORD SEARCH – SHEET #7
GENESIS – REVELATION

There are 66 books in the bible – 39 Old Testament Books and 27 New Testament Books.

COMMANDMENTS
CREATION
DAY OF ATONEMENT
DEITY
DOMINION
EGYPTIANS
EXODUS
FELLOWSHIP
GENEALOGY
GIDEON
GLORY
JERICHO
JESUS
JUDAH
PATRIARCHAL
PENTECOST
PREACHED
RAHAB
REMNANT
RENEW
SPIRITUALLY
TESTAMENT
TRUMPETS
UNLEAVENED
WORSHIP
ZIGGURAT

```
D O M I N I O N O K M L E V P
E L J E R I C H O F Q G R W A
I I R F E L L O W S H I P I T
T Z A E R V H G U J U D A H R
Y U N L E A V E N E D S G O I
Z I G G U R A T A G B F E S A
L X I N A G L H D L E L T S R
C L P R E A C H E D N N J W C
R M B R G A Q R P T E V D H
E A G I D E O N H M L E A X A
A E B R A J H S D P K R Y U L
T E S T A M E N T N A S O E Z
I H A R K I A S I W S H F L E
O R I N C M S G L O R Y A I G
N E C T M R I N E R E L T A Y
N A M O L J E L T S R N O B P
G I C K P E L Y C H L E N P T
E H E L U S I E L I P R E S I
N R A N S U A P O P U A M T A
E X O D U S B I D A N H E R N
A T P M T R E N E W H A N U S
L Q N O E L I A S A P B T M W
O R P E N T E C O S T E P E L
G L I S H A M A M E L T C E L
Y Y R E M N A N T H I R A T F
N S P I R I T U A L L Y D D
```

WORD SEARCH – SHEET #8
THE NUMBER TWELVE – GOVERNMENTAL PERFECTION

The number twelve is used one hundred eighty-seven times in the bible, Genesis (8), Exodus (7), Leviticus (1), Numbers (17), Deuteronomy (1), Joshua (11), Judges (2), 2 Samuel (4), 1 Kings (30), 2 Kings (2), 1 Chronicles (26), 2 Chronicles (7), Ezra (6), Nehemiah (2), Esther (1), Psalms (1), Jeremiah (2), Ezekiel (3), Daniel (1), Matthew (13), Mark (14), Luke (13), John (6), Acts (5), 1 Corinthians (1), James (1) and Revelation (22). One Old Testament book has 12 chapters. Do you know which book that is? Hint: Book tells a story of a young man in a lion's den.

ADBON
APOSTLES
BULLS
CAKES
CHURCHES
DEBORAH
DISCIPLES
EHUD
ELON
FOUNDATIONS
FRUITS
GATES
GIDEON
GOVERNORS
HEMORRHAGE
IZBAN
JAIR
JEPHTHAH
LAMPSTANDS
LEGION OF ANGELS
MINOR PROPHETS
MONTHS
OTHNIEL
OXEN
PRINCES
RAMS
SAMSON   SPIES   TRIBES
SCROLLS   STARS   YEARS
SHAMGAR   STONES
SIGNS   TOLA

```
O T H N I E L L J G A T E S V I
A L E N M H R A M S J G R W Z
H I N D A U F Y B C R S D I B A
I E A Y R T X L I M Y E A R S H
G I D E O N A S A G B M E L H
E R I N A O M O D M E G I M W E
J L N E U S P N T O L A I N L
E L O N G A S S P N A R N L
P A G I E M T D H T L E I O L
H T O S E P O N M T S A E E P H
T O S E P O N M T S A E E R P
H H A R K E N D S R W S M E F R
A D B O N E S O I G I O I D O U
H E C T A R I N B K G R D P H U
C H U R C H E S E U N R N O H N
D I S C I P L E S A S H O E T D
S H E L U M I E L O P A F T A
A P O S T L E S O X U G A S T
I A V T I A B P D E N E N A I O
C T P O T R K I E N H D G I O
E Q N N E L L E S A B H E N N S
C A K E S E P S C R O L L S S
E L I S G O V E R N O R S A L
B U L L S I S T A R S R A L V
P R I N C E S E L F R U I T S
```

ANSWERS TO WORD SEARCH

WORD SEARCH – SHEET #9

BABYLON
CHRIST
DIVISION
FAITH
FATHER
GRACE
GOODNESS
HARVEST
IDOLATRY
INIQUITY
JUDGMENT
LORD
MESSIAH
PERFECTION
PRECEPTS
PRIDE
PROMISE
REBELLION
RECONCILIATION
REDEMPTION
RIGHTEOUSNESS
SAYING
STATUTES
TABERNACLE
TEMPTATION
TESTIMONIES
TRANSGRESSION
VALUE
VENGEANCE
VICTORY
VINEYARD
WAY
WORD
WORSHIP

T	E	S	T	I	M	O	N	I	E	S	L	J	V	P
A	L	A	N	M	D	A	N	P	F	T	F	U	W	R
R	I	Y	D	W	O	R	D	E	C	A	A	D	I	E
I	Z	I	E	A	V	H	D	R	J	T	I	G	H	C
G	U	N	R	Y	E	T	I	F	Y	U	T	M	O	E
H	R	G	O	T	N	A	J	E	G	T	H	E	L	P
T	X	I	C	A	G	G	H	C	L	E	L	N	S	T
E	I	N	H	B	E	O	M	T	O	S	O	T	W	S
O	D	B	R	E	A	O	R	I	T	A	V	N	O	T
U	O	A	I	R	N	D	L	O	R	D	E	A	X	P
S	L	B	S	N	C	N	S	N	P	K	R	H	U	R
N	A	Y	T	A	E	E	M	E	S	S	I	A	H	O
E	T	L	R	C	I	S	S	I	T	V	F	O	L	M
S	R	O	N	L	E	S	O	M	E	I	A	N	I	I
S	Y	N	T	E	R	I	N	E	M	N	T	M	N	S
G	A	D	W	O	R	S	H	I	P	E	H	O	I	E
V	I	C	K	P	O	K	Y	C	T	Y	E	B	Q	U
I	H	E	G	V	A	L	U	E	A	A	R	Y	U	G
C	R	A	R	S	F	A	P	O	T	R	L	D	I	P
T	A	V	A	I	A	B	I	D	I	D	T	I	T	S
O	T	P	C	P	R	I	D	E	O	H	D	V	Y	T
R	E	D	E	M	P	T	I	O	N	P	H	I	N	W
Y	X	H	A	R	V	E	S	T	N	S	E	S	F	E
E	R	E	C	O	N	C	I	L	I	A	T	I	O	N
M	Y	R	E	B	E	L	L	I	O	N	R	O	L	V
T	R	A	N	S	G	R	E	S	S	I	O	N	L	E

WORD SEARCH – SHEET #10

DAVID
DAYS
DELIVERANCE
ELIJAH
FORTY
GOLIATH
HOREB
HUMILIATION
JEHOVAH
JESUS
JUDGES
JUSTICE
LAID
MEDIATOR
MT CARMEL
NIGHTS
PROBATION
RIGHTEOUS
RIVAL
SAINT
SALVATION
SAUL
SCRIPTURES
SERVITUDE
SIN
SOLOMON
SPIRIT
STRIPES
TEMPTED
THIRTY
TROUBLES
WORD
YEARS

S	O	L	O	M	O	N	J	O	K	D	A	V	I	D					
A	L	E	N	M	D	I	N	J	F	A	G	R	W	S					
U	I	N	D	A	L	G	Y	U	C	Y	E	A	R	S					
E	O	A	R	T	X	T	I	T	Y	R	M	G	O	P					
E	L	I	J	A	H	S	J	I	G	I	P	L	R	O					
R	A	N	S	T	R	I	P	E	S	H	I	D	W	B					
U	T	B	U	G	A	Q	S	P	T	T	A	G	X	A					
T	H	G	S	E	L	G	F	H	I	E	D	E	U	T					
E	E	B	R	A	A	H	I	R	P	O	O	S	H	I					
M	C	S	I	N	I	U	R	A	N	U	R	H	E	O					
P	H	A	R	K	D	T	I	B	W	R	Y	O	L	N					
E	C	D	E	L	I	V	E	R	A	N	C	E	W	U					
D	A	S	E	R	V	I	T	U	D	E	N	O	B	X					
N	I	C	K	P	O	R	I	V	A	L	E	B	P	U					
M	T	C	A	R	M	E	L	L	N	P	W	O	R	D					
T	J	A	N	S	A	L	V	A	T	I	O	N	R	P					
I	E	V	U	I	A	B	S	O	M	S	A	I	N	T					
C	H	P	M	T	H	I	R	T	Y	H	D	F	I	W					
H	O	N	O	K	Y	U	A	S	W	P	H	K	N	F					
O	V	H	U	M	I	L	I	A	T	I	O	N	E	R					
R	A	I	S	T	R	O	U	B	L	E	S	C	A	R					
E	H	R	W	Q	L	S	P	A	H	I	R	A	V	T					
B	A	S	C	R	I	P	T	U	R	E	S	W	L	Y					

WORD SEARCH – SHEET #11

WORDS BEGINNING WITH THE LETTER "W"

WAGES
WALLS
WAR
WATCHMAN
WATER
WATERPOTS
WEDDING
WEEK
WEIGHT
WELLS
WHALE
WHEAT
WHISPERER
WIDOW
WIDOWER
WIFE
WILDERNESS
WILLOW
WINDOW
WINE
WINEBIBBER
WINNOW
WINTER
WISE
WITNESS
WIZARD
WOE
WOLF
WOMAN
WONDERFUL
WOOL
WORD
WORM
WORMWOOD
WORSHIP
WREATH
WRITE
WROUGHT

W	A	T	E	R	P	O	T	S	K	W	H	A	L	E
O	L	E	N	M	D	I	N	P	F	R	G	R	Y	S
R	I	N	D	W	A	L	L	S	C	E	E	A	X	S
M	W	O	R	M	V	H	D	U	J	A	D	A	E	A
W	O	N	D	E	R	F	U	L	Y	T	S	G	M	P
O	R	I	J	A	H	U	J	A	W	H	E	A	T	R
O	S	W	A	G	E	S	H	D	I	E	W	U	S	O
D	H	A	S	T	C	I	P	E	N	N	I	D	W	B
U	I	T	W	A	R	Q	R	P	T	A	Z	G	I	A
T	P	C	S	E	L	G	D	H	E	L	A	E	N	W
E	E	H	R	A	S	B	W	O	R	D	R	S	D	O
M	W	M	W	E	I	G	H	T	N	A	D	H	O	R
P	I	A	I	K	D	T	S	I	W	E	E	K	W	T
T	N	N	L	W	I	D	O	W	E	R	N	N	I	H
E	E	C	L	E	L	I	V	E	R	A	N	C	E	Y
H	B	S	O	B	W	I	F	E	W	E	N	O	B	X
S	I	C	W	R	I	T	E	V	I	L	E	B	P	U
S	B	C	O	P	N	E	W	L	N	P	W	I	N	D
E	B	A	L	S	E	W	H	O	N	W	O	O	L	P
N	E	V	F	I	A	I	I	S	O	I	M	I	O	W
R	R	P	M	T	H	D	S	S	W	S	A	F	I	E
E	Q	N	W	O	E	O	P	E	A	E	N	K	N	L
D	R	H	U	M	I	W	E	N	T	I	O	N	F	L
L	W	A	T	E	R	M	R	T	E	L	T	C	A	S
I	Y	R	W	Q	L	S	E	I	H	I	R	A	L	T
W	R	O	U	G	H	T	R	W	E	D	D	I	N	G

WORD SEARCH – SHEET #12

ABISHAI
ABNER
ARMORBEARER
BATHSHEBA
BOAZ
COMMANDER
DEBORAH
ELI
GIDEON
GENERAL
JOAB
JONATHAN
KING
MERAB
MICHAL
MILLER
MUSICIAN
NAOMI
NATHAN
PIPERS
RELIGION
SAMSON
SAMUEL
SAUL
TEMPLE
TESTAMENT
THRONE
THUMMIM
TIBERIAS
URIAH
VASHNI
VILE
ZERUIAH
ZETHAM
ZETHAN
ZETHAR
ZIBA

B	O	A	Z	X	O	N	J	O	T	D	A	Z	I	N
A	L	E	N	M	D	I	O	P	I	E	G	V	W	A
T	I	U	D	A	L	G	A	B	B	B	E	A	R	O
H	G	J	R	R	V	H	B	Z	E	O	D	S	H	M
S	O	A	R	I	X	C	I	E	R	R	S	H	O	I
H	V	I	J	A	T	J	T	I	A	B	N	E	R	R
E	L	I	E	A	O	H	D	H	A	H	L	I	S	O
B	A	N	S	T	R	R	P	A	S	N	O	D	W	C
A	T	B	U	G	B	O	A	R	T	A	V	G	O	O
T	K	I	N	G	L	N	D	T	H	U	M	M	I	M
E	E	B	R	X	A	E	N	E	R	K	R	S	U	M
M	I	L	L	E	R	U	M	A	V	I	L	E	W	A
P	H	A	R	K	D	T	G	E	N	E	R	A	L	I
T	R	I	N	S	A	M	S	O	N	P	Q	N	I	D
E	E	C	M	U	S	I	C	I	A	N	N	Z	E	E
D	A	Z	E	R	U	I	A	H	D	E	N	I	B	R
N	A	T	H	A	N	R	I	V	A	L	E	B	P	U
P	Z	I	B	A	H	A	N	Z	E	T	H	A	N	A
I	E	A	N	S	F	A	T	E	M	P	L	E	Y	B
P	T	V	U	I	H	B	U	Z	Z	I	A	H	V	I
E	H	P	M	T	W	I	M	I	C	H	A	L	I	S
R	A	N	A	R	M	O	R	B	E	A	R	E	R	H
S	M	N	G	M	R	E	L	I	G	I	O	N	S	A
R	O	B	Y	H	A	M	E	R	A	B	T	C	A	I
J	T	E	S	T	A	M	E	N	T	I	R	A	U	T
P	G	I	D	E	O	N	X	S	A	M	U	E	L	Y

ANSWERS TO WORD SEARCH

WORD SEARCH – SHEET #13

AARON
ASP
BLOODY
BOILS
CATTLE
DARKNESS
DEATH
DUST
EARTHQUAKES
EGYPT
EGYPTIANS
ERUPTION
FLIES
FROGS
GNATS
HAIL
ISRAEL
ISRAELITES
LEPROSY
LIVESTOCK
LOCUSTS
MIRIAM
MOSES
PESTILENCE
PHAROAH
PRAYERS
RUGGED
SANDSTORMS   SUN
SERPANT   TIDAL WAVE
STAFF   VOLCANO
STRONG   WATER

WORD SEARCH – SHEET #14
BOOK OF MARK

BAPTIZE
BELIEVE
CAMEL
CAPERNAUM
DEMONS
DOCTRINE
EUTHEOS
FISHERMAN
FORERUNNER
GALILEAN
GODHEAD
GOSPEL
HEAVEN
HOLY
HUSBANDMEN
LEPER
MASTER
MINISTRY
NAZARETH
PARABLE
PRIEST
PROCLAIM
REGION
REPENT
SABBATH
SATAN
SCRIBES   TESTIFY
SPIRIT   WILDERNESS
SYNAGOGUE   ZEBEDEE

WORD SEARCH – SHEET #16
THE BOOK OF EPHESIANS

ABOUND
APOSTLE
BELOVED
BLESSED
CHRIST
CHRISTIAN
DISPENSATION
DOMINION
EPHESUS
FORGIVENESS
FOUNDATION
FULLNESS
GLORY
GRACE
GREATNESS
HEAVEN
INHERITANCE
POWER
PRAYER
PREDESTINED
PRINCIPALITY
REDEMPTION
REVELATION
RIGHTEOUSNESS
SAINT
SALVATION
SPIRITUAL
STRENGTH   UNDERSTANDING
SUFFICIENT   UNMERITED
TESTING   WORLD
TRANSFORM   WORTHY

WORD SEARCH – SHEET #15
BOOK OF PROVERBS

AUTHOR
DESPISE
DIDACTIC
DISCRETION
ENIGMA
EQUITY
FORSAKE
GRACEFUL
HOUSES
INNOCENT
INSTRUCTION
JUDGMENT
JUSTICE
KNOWLEDGE
PARALLELISM
PHILOSOPHER
POETICAL
POSSESSIONS
PRECIOUS
PROVERB
PRUDENCE
PURSE
SCIENTIST
SECTION
SHEOL
SINNERS
SOLOMON
SONGS
SPOIL   WISDOM
SWALLOW   WISE
VAIN   WONDER
WALK   WORDS
     WORLD

ANSWERS TO WORD SEARCH

WORD SEARCH – SHEET #17

ALTAR
ANOINTING
ARK
ATONEMENT
AVENGER
BAAL
BLESSING
BLOOD
BREASTPLATE
CALF
CEREMONY
CHIEF PRIEST
CIRCUMCISION
CLEANLINESS
CLERGY
COMMUNION
COMMUNITY
CONGREGATION
CURTAIN
DEFILEMENT
DRINK
EPHOD
FEASTS
FREEWILL
HOLY
INCENSE
KINSMEN
OIL
ORDINANCE
PENTECOST
PHYLACTERY
PREACHER
RELATIONSHIP
RULER
SACRIFICIAL
SOUL
WISDOM

```
A N O I N T I N G K D R I N K
T L E N M D I N P F E S R W I
O I C U R T A I N C F A A C N
N G J O R V H D U L I C A I S
E O I R T X T I M E L R G R M
M L I J A H S J A R E I J C E
E I I E B L O O D G M F U U N
N A V E N G E R U Y E I B M B
T T B U G A Q R P L N C R C C
W I S D O M G D H I T I E A A
O E C E R E M O N Y K A A S L
R O S E P I U M A N A L S I F
D H C H I E F P R I E S T O N
I R I C O M M U N I O N P N B
N C L E A N L I N E S S L P A
A A S E R E I T U D Y N A R A
N I C K R O R I V A L E T E L
C O N G R E G A T I O N E A D
E R E L A T I O N S H I P C P
I A P E N T E C O S T N I H N
F B L E S S I N G B H D F E T
E Q N O E P H Y L A C T E R Y
A L T A R I L I A T I O M F O
S L C O M M U N I T Y U C A R
T Y R F R E E W I L L R A R K
S A E P H O D T I N C E N S E
```

WORD SEARCH – SHEET #18

BLESS
CHURCH
CHRIST
CORONATION
DEACON
ELDERS
EVANGELIST
EXCOMMUNICATION
FELLOWSHIP
GENTILE
GREEK
HOLY
HUMANITY
HYMN
JESUS
JEW
JUDAISM
LEADER
MISSIONARY
ORDINATION
OVERSEER
PHARISEE
SACREMENT
SADDUCEE
SANHEDRIN
SAMARITAN
SANCTUARY
SECT
SEER
SHRINE
SONG
TABLET
TEACHER
TETRACH
VICTORY

```
E X C O M M U N I C A T I O N
V L E S I D I B L E S S R R S
A I N D S A C R E M E N T D A
N G A N S L E L D E R S P N H
E N L C O T I M Y E S G I N E
N L C O T L H Y M N L I E D D
L T E N N V J U D A I S M T I
I I A W A O I P E S N O C I R
S L D P R K Q G R E E K T O N
T E E U Y L D E A C O N O I N
E C R V I C T O R Y K R V U E
O O S S A M A R I T A N S P O
V R A R S E C T I W S P B H N
E O R N C R T E T R A C H A U
R N A D E L I V E L A V J R S
S A D D U C E E A D J N T I E
E T I K P O R I C A E E A S E
E I I A A R M E L H N S W B P
R O N H O L Y P E P U C L E N
I N T U I A B D R M S H E O R
C S A N C T U A R Y H R T I R
H Q N O E C H U R C H I K N D
O R H U M A N I T Y I S N F O
R L I S H R I N E L T L A R T
E Y R W Q S E E R H I R A L T
F E L L O W S H I P E S J E W
```

WORD SEARCH – SHEET #19

ABIJAH
ANGEL
BARREN
CLEAN
COMMANDMENTS
CONCEIVE
COUSINS
DAY SPRING
DISOBEDIENT
ELIZABETH
EXCELLENT
EYEWITNESSES
FAVOR
GABRIEL
GLAD TIDINGS
GOOD WORKS
HEART
HEROD
HOLY SPIRIT
JESUS
JOHN
LAW
MINISTRY
PREACH
PRIESTHOOD
PROMISE
PULPIT
SOCIAL
SUFFER
THEOPHILUS
VICTORY
ZACHARIAS

```
A B I J A H P E G V D R I N Z
T L E N M D W S P I I P R W A
O I C O U S I N S C S R E C A
C Z J E S U S D U T O I X I H
O O A R H E A R T E S E C I A
M I N I S T R Y A R E S E C R
M N I E X L U O D Y D T L L D
A A V C N G E R E U I H L D A
N G O O D W O R K S E O E A S
D Y G N E L L G D H I N O N C
M A C C R E M O N Y T D T S A
E H L E P R E A C H A S S P L
N O R I G F P H L E F T P R F
T L I V C P U L P I T A P I D
S Y L E A N L I N E S V W N B
A S U F F E R W V X E O H G A
N P C K P O W E R C L R R P R
C I N G R H C A U P O N E R R
E R I A S E A P R O M I S E E
I I P B N R E C O S T N I O N
F T P R S O C I A L H T W Y K
E Q N I E D L V L A O J O H N
A N G E L I E L I Z A B E T H
S L C L G L A D T I D I N G S
E Y E W I T N E S S E S A R K
T H E O P H I L U S C E L A W
```

VICTORY
ZACHARIAS

WORD SEARCH – SHEET #20

ADORATION
AMEN
BENEDICTION
CHALLENGE
COMMEMORATION
COMMEND
CONFESSION
DECISION
DOXOLOGY
EDIFICATION
ENCOURAGEMENT
ENDURANCE
ENLIGHTENMENT
EQUIPMENT
EVANGELISM
GIVING
GLORIFY
GRACE
GROWTH
HAPPY
HEART
HONOR
HOSPITALITY
HYMNAL
LAUGH
LOVE
MEDITATION
MERCY
PERSEVERANCE
PRAISE
PRAY
PRIORITY
REJOICE
STUDY
TESTIFY
TESTIMONY
THANKSGIVING

```
T B C A D O R A T I O N P C E
H Q O H X G R A C E F B E N L
A Z N Y C O M M E N D U R M I
N D F M R W C G L P X Y S M G
K O E N E J P R A I S E E E H
S X S A J M R X R G W N V M T
G O S L O G I V I N G D E O T
I L I P H O N O R O U R A T E
I G N Q G E V I F A A E N N M
N Y W P J P T L M P E N C I M
G L O R I F Y A E P E C E O E
S K C O H R C X N Y D D T N N
E V U I M E R C Y P I M E D T
Q T R S W Q X H K L C E D M E
U W D E C I S I O N T N I F V
I O V I H E A R T R I T F D A
P R A Y A K L O P W O T I I N
M S Z O L A U G H Z N E C I G
E H C P L O V E S B V S A A E
N I I M E D S T U D Y T T I L
T P X J N C X V B P J I I I S
W L E D G R O W T H I F O N M
I Z R T E S T I M O N Y N N M
H O S P I T A L I T Y P M E R
E N C O U R A G E M E N T W C
```

PRAY   TESTIFY
PRIORITY   TESTIMONY
REJOICE   THANKSGIVING
STUDY

ANSWERS TO WORD SEARCH

WORD SEARCH – SHEET #21

ASSURANCE
CELEBRATION
DENIAL
DETERMINATION
DISCIPLINE
EXAMINATION
FRIENDSHIP
GUIDANCE
INQUIRE
JUST
LIFT
LONG
PROGRESS
RECLAIM
REFORMATION
RELIGION
REMEMBER
RENEWAL
RENUNCIATION
RESPECT
RESPONSIBLE
RIGHTEOUSNESS
SELF-SACRIFICE
SPIRITUAL
STRIVE
THEOLOGY
TITHE

VALUABLE
WARFARE
WATCHFULNESS

WHOLESOME
WITHSTAND
WITNESS

WONDERFUL

S	P	I	R	I	T	U	A	L	K	D	R	I	N		D
P	L	E	N	M	D	I	N	O	F	E	G	R	W		E
K	R	E	L	I	G	I	O	N	C	F	L	I	F	T	
F	G	J	E	R	V	H	D	G	J	I	D	X	I		E
S	E	L	F	S	A	C	R	I	F	I	C	E	J	R	
A	S	S	U	R	A	N	C	E	G	E	F	G	C		M
R	T	W	E	E	L	O	O	D	L	M	L	U	U		
E	R	A	W	F	R	I	E	N	D	S	H	I	P	N	
C	I	R	H	O	I	R	R	P	I	W	V	D	C		A
L	V	F	O	R	G	E	D	H	S	O	E	A	I		T
A	E	A	L	M	H	S	O	N	C	N	R	N	N		
I	O	R	E	A	T	P	M	A	I	D	S	C	Q	O	
M	H	E	S	T	E	O	P	R	P	E	R	E	U		N
P	W	T	O	I	O	N	R	E	L	R	E	V	I		B
W	I	H	M	O	U	S	O	N	I	F	S	A	R	R	
A	T	E	E	N	S	I	G	E	N	U	P	L	E	E	
T	H	O	K	P	N	B	R	W	E	L	E	U	P	M	
C	S	L	G	R	E	L	E	A	I	O	C	A	R	M	
H	T	O	N	S	S	E	S	L	P	U	T	B	R	M	
F	A	G	E	N	S	J	S	O	S	Z	N	L	O	B	
U	N	Y	M	T	H	I	R	T	I	T	H	E	J		
L	D	N	O	E	P	D	E	N	I	A	L	E	U	R	
N	C	E	L	E	B	R	A	T	I	O	N	S	S	O	
E	X	A	M	I	N	A	T	I	O	N	U	C	T	R	
S	Y	R	F	R	E	E	K	W	I	T	N	E	S	S	
S	R	E	N	U	N	C	I	A	T	I	O	N	S	E	

WORD SEARCH – SHEET #22

AFFLUENCE
APOSTASY
ASTOLOGY
ATHEISM
DECEPTION
DISCOURAGEMENT
DISHONESTY
DISOBEDIENCE
DISTRUST
DOUBT
ENEMY
ENVY
EVIL
FAILURE
FAITHLESSNESS
FAVORITISM
FOLLY
FOOLS
GRUDGE
LEGALISM
LIBERTINISM
LIES
LUST
MATERIALISM
MOCKERY
NEGLECT

D	L	I	B	E	R	T	I	N	I	S	M	I	N	F
I	I	E	N	M	D	I	N	P	E	E	G	R	W	A
S	I	S	U	F	T	A	I	N	C	G	E	A	C	V
O	G	J	C	R	O	H	D	U	J	R	L	A	I	O
B	O	A	R	O	X	O	I	M	Y	U	S	E	R	R
E	L	I	F	G	E	I	T	Q	U	A	G	E	J	I
D	I	I	E	T	L	R	O	S	L	G	L	U	U	T
I	A	J	E	H	F	E	A	E	S	E	O	B	M	I
E	V	I	L	E	A	Q	F	G	T	N	V	R	C	S
N	H	G	E	I	I	G	F	H	E	T	E	E	I	M
C	E	C	G	A	M	E	L	N	Y	M	R	A	S	C
E	O	S	A	M	U	K	U	A	N	A	E	S	I	L
D	H	C	L	I	R	Y	E	R	I	E	S	N	O	I
I	R	I	I	C	E	W	N	T	I	O	N	A	T	E
N	C	L	S	E	N	L	C	N	E	S	S	P	E	S
A	A	S	M	R	V	I	E	U	D	E	N	O	Z	A
N	I	C	K	D	I	S	T	R	U	S	T	P	P	D
C	O	N	G	A	S	T	O	L	O	G	Y	T	E	I
M	A	T	E	R	I	A	L	I	S	M	L	A	N	S
I	A	P	K	N	T	E	C	M	S	D	N	S	E	H
F	T	D	E	C	E	P	T	I	O	N	D	Y	M	O
E	Q	N	O	Y	P	H	Y	U	A	C	T	E	Y	N
A	J	T	L	R	I	L	B	A	T	I	K	N	F	F
S	X	L	U	M	M	T	B	I	T	Y	U	E	A	S
T	O	R	S	R	E	N	V	Y	C	F	R	A	R	T
F	A	I	T	H	L	E	S	S	N	E	S	S	W	Y

WORD SEARCH – SHEET #23

BLAMELESSNESS
BOLDNESS
CHARACTER
CHASTITY
CHILDLIKENESS
CHRIST
COMMITMENT
CONFIDENCE
CONFORMITY
CONSECRATION
COURAGE
DEDICATION
DEPENDENCE
DEVOTION
DISCERN
DISCIPLINE
DOCTRINE
EARNESTNESS
ETHICS
FAITHFULNESS
FRUITFULNESS
GENTLENESS
GODLINESS
HOLINESS
HONESTY
HUMILITY
LOYAL
STAUNCH
UNERRING

B	L	A	M	E	L	E	S	S	N	E	S	S	N	K
O	L	E	N	A	D	E	V	O	T	I	O	N	F	I
L	I	C	U	R	T	A	D	N	C	F	E	R	A	N
D	G	H	E	N	V	H	O	U	J	I	D	A	I	S
N	O	R	D	E	D	I	C	A	T	I	O	N	T	M
E	L	I	S	S	H	S	T	A	G	E	F	J	H	E
S	C	S	T	T	L	O	R	D	L	M	L	U	F	F
S	H	T	A	N	G	E	I	E	S	E	O	B	U	R
T	A	B	U	E	A	Q	N	P	T	N	C	R	L	U
D	S	G	N	S	L	G	E	H	I	C	O	G	N	I
E	T	C	C	S	E	M	O	N	M	O	M	E	E	T
P	I	C	H	D	I	S	C	E	R	N	M	N	S	F
E	T	H	I	C	S	P	R	I	F	I	I	T	S	U
N	Y	I	H	O	N	E	S	T	Y	I	T	L	O	L
D	C	L	C	A	N	I	I	N	L	D	M	E	E	
E	A	D	O	U	V	I	T	A	C	E	E	N	D	I
N	H	L	N	N	O	R	Y	V	O	N	N	E	I	S
C	D	I	F	E	E	D	A	T	U	C	T	S	S	
E	L	K	O	R	L	A	P	D	R	E	L	S	C	P
I	I	E	R	R	T	E	C	O	A	T	N	I	I	
F	E	N	M	I	H	I	R	T	G	H	D	F	P	T
E	E	E	I	N	P	H	Y	L	E	C	T	E	L	Y
A	S	S	T	G	O	D	L	I	N	E	S	S	I	O
W	S	S	Y	M	H	U	M	I	L	I	T	Y	N	R
T	Y	R	F	R	E	C	H	A	R	A	C	T	E	R
C	O	N	S	E	C	R	E	T	I	O	N	N	S	E

WORD SEARCH – SHEET #24

ADORATION
CALMNESS
FORBEARANCE
FORTITUDE
GENTLE
GOODWILL
INNOCENCE
INSIGHT
INTOLERANCE
JOY
KINDNESS
LOVE
LOYALTY
MEEKNESS
MERCIFULNESS
MODERNATION
MODESTY
MORALITY
NURTURE
ORTHODOXY
PATIENCE
PERCEPTION
PERFECTION
PIETY
PURITY
QUIETNESS
READINESS
RECEPTIVE
RELIABLE
RELISH

RESTRAINT
REVERENCE
SEPARATION
SERVANT

STOICISM
TRUSTWORTHY
VIRTUE
WARMHEARTEDNESS

WARMTH
WORSHIP

T	R	E	V	E	R	E	N	C	E	X	N	W	J	M
R	E	C	A	L	M	N	E	S	S	B	U	A	H	O
U	C	W	Z	L	O	Y	A	L	T	Y	R	R	C	D
S	E	R	E	S	T	R	A	I	N	T	T	M	V	E
T	P	E	R	C	E	P	T	I	O	N	U	T	P	R
W	T	Y	S	R	T	A	L	O	V	E	R	H	K	N
O	I	F	G	E	I	T	Q	U	A	G	E	J	I	A
R	V	O	X	C	M	I	F	S	E	R	V	A	N	T
T	E	R	F	G	O	E	I	A	V	N	H	W	D	I
H	Y	R	H	M	O	N	N	P	I	E	T	Y	N	O
Y	P	E	R	F	E	C	T	I	O	N	P	M	E	N
W	U	A	E	O	S	E	O	R	G	D	E	S	X	
O	R	R	A	R	T	R	L	T	T	E	Y	E	S	M
S	I	A	D	T	Y	E	E	O	H	N	S	K	G	E
H	T	C	N	T	D	I	R	A	C	D	L	E	O	R
I	N	E	E	U	F	S	N	I	O	E	R	S	D	C
P	D	X	S	S	E	C	B	E	M	Y	J	R	B	I
U	P	T	S	E	C	B	E	M	Y	J	R	B	I	U
M	O	R	A	L	I	T	Y	P	O	K	A	D	L	L
Y	Q	Z	X	Y	I	N	S	I	G	H	T	M	L	L
A	D	O	R	A	T	I	O	N	V	W	I	F	R	E
R	E	L	I	A	B	L	E	Y	S	X	O	K	W	S
V	I	R	T	U	E	Q	U	I	E	T	N	E	S	S
W	A	R	M	H	E	A	R	T	E	D	N	E	S	S
I	N	N	O	C	E	N	C	E	F	G	X	J	O	Y

ANSWERS TO WORD SEARCH

WORD SEARCH – SHEET #25

F	I	D	O	L	A	T	R	Y	K	F	G	P	H	U	
O	P	P	R	E	S	S	I	O	N	L	B	O	C	N	
R	X	M	H	Y	P	O	C	R	I	S	Y	L	W	O	
G	J	Q	X	S	H	A	M	E	F	U	L	Y	V	F	
E	P	E	R	S	E	C	U	T	I	O	N	T	O	R	
T	Y	J	E	A	L	O	U	S	L	Y	R	H	P	G	
F	O	R	G	I	V	E	N	E	S	S	D	E	P	I	
U	N	S	E	L	F	I	S	H	I	K	P	I	O	V	
L	V	T	P	R	E	M	O	R	S	E	F	S	S	E	
N	H	U	N	G	R	A	T	E	F	U	L	M	I	N	
E	P	R	E	S	U	M	P	T	I	O	N	J	T	E	
S	K	E	M	P	A	T	H	Y	H	D	B	W	I	S	
S	U	P	E	R	S	T	I	T	I	O	N	O	O	S	
G	N	B	M	E	U	H	G	M	V	P	C	R	N	J	
U	D	Y	E	J	S	A	K	W	F	Z	A	T	C	H	
W	E	S	E	U	P	N	I	C	E	G	R	H	P	E	
O	R	P	K	D	I	K	N	O	Y	U	E	I	H	R	
R	S	I	N	I	C	F	D	G	V	I	X	N	C	E	
L	T	T	E	C	I	U	N	B	E	L	I	E	F	S	
D	A	E	S	E	O	L	K	J	D	T	K	S	O	Y	
L	N	F	S	Z	N	B	R	W	I	S	E	S	L	M	
I	D	U	W	Q	P	R	I	D	E	U	V	T	L	I	
N	I	L	V	U	L	G	A	R	I	T	Y	P	Y	F	
E	N	D	C	O	N	S	C	I	E	N	C	E	G	E	
S	G	K	J	I	D	G	E	N	E	R	O	U	S	A	
S	L	O	T	H	F	U	L	N	E	S	S	W	I	R	

CARE
CONSCIENCE
EMPATHY
FEAR
FOLLY
FORGETFULNESS
FORGIVENESS
GENEROUS
GRATEFUL
GUILT
HERESY
IDOLATRY
JEALOUSLY
MEEKNESS
NICE
OPPRESSION
OPPOSITION
PERSECUTION
POLYTHEISM
PREJUDICE
PRESUMPTION
PRIDE
REMORSE
SHAMEFUL
SLOTHFULNESS
SPITEFUL
SUSPICION
SUPERSTITION
THANKFUL
UNBELIEF

UNDERSTANDING
UNFORGIVENESS
UNSELFISH
VULGARITY

WISE
WORLDLINESS
WORTHINESS

ANSWERS TO CRYPTOGRAMS – SHEET #1

1. JLLS KYS HCZTJFW TB WFD QLZS. (Psalm 25:8)

G	O	O	D
J	L	L	S

A	N	D
K	Y	S

U	P	R	I	G	H	T
H	C	Z	T	J	F	W

I	S
T	B

T	H	E
W	F	D

L	O	R	D
Q	L	Z	S

2. M SO BRY PMJRB TN BRY CTKPU. (John 9:5)

I
M

A	M
S	O

T	H	E
B	R	Y

L	I	G	H	T
P	M	J	R	B

O	F
T	N

T	H	E
B	R	Y

W	O	R	L	D
C	T	K	P	U

3. TWY LM PLTOR SKY LK OLX ROGDG LM KWROLKT YSDF. (I John 1:5)

G	O	D
T	W	Y

I	S
L	M

L	I	G	H	T
P	L	T	O	R

A	N	D
S	K	Y

I	N
L	K

H	I	M
O	L	X

T	H	E	R	E
R	O	G	D	G

I	S
L	M

N	O	T	H	I	N	G
K	W	R	O	L	K	T

D	A	R	K
Y	S	D	F

4. SKE WBL ELDGEC KS PMZ MP CLGWB. (Romans 6:23)

F	O	R
S	K	E

T	H	E
W	B	L

R	E	W	A	R	D
E	L	D	G	E	C

O	F
K	S

S	I	N
P	M	Z

I	S
M	P

D	E	A	T	H
C	L	G	W	B

5. TKS PCF IK DF LFCNFVI FYFE PG TKSC NPIXFC ME XFPYFE MG LFCNFVI. (Matthew 5:48)

Y	O	U
T	K	S

A	R	E
P	C	F

T	O
I	K

B	E
D	F

P	E	R	F	E	C	T
L	F	C	N	F	V	I

E	V	E	N
F	Y	F	E

A	S
P	G

Y	O	U	R
T	K	S	C

F	A	T	H	E	R
N	P	I	X	F	C

I	N
M	E

H	E	A	V	E	N
X	F	P	Y	F	E

I	S
M	G

P	E	R	F	E	C	T
L	F	C	N	F	V	I

6. SFY BSS KPW CP IF CPTF ZMYG SPZF. (I Corinthians 16:14)

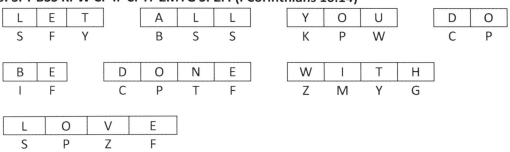

L	E	T
S	F	Y

A	L	L
B	S	S

Y	O	U
K	P	W

D	O
C	P

B	E
I	F

D	O	N	E
C	P	T	F

W	I	T	H
Z	M	Y	G

L	O	V	E
S	P	Z	F

7. CET VF VLPM DN CLGXY, WEX DN HGZYX. (2 Corinthians 5:7)

F	O	R
C	E	T

W	E
V	F

W	A	L	K
V	L	P	M

B	Y
D	N

F	A	I	T	H
C	L	G	X	Y

N	O	T
W	E	X

B	Y
D	N

S	I	G	H	T
H	G	Z	Y	X

180

ANSWERS TO CRYPTOGRAMS – SHEET #3

8. WNE TPMSS XNB BYWZB BPY SNGH WNEG DNH. (Matthew 4:7)

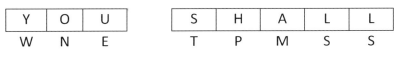

| Y O U | S H A L L | N O T |
| W N E | T P M S S | X N B |

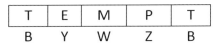

| T E M P T | T H E | L O R D |
| B Y W Z B | B P Y | S N G H |

| Y O U R | G O D |
| W N E G | D N H |

9. SALABF CHS FTA YUBZGHD HC TAWNAB UK WF TWBG. (Matthew 3:2)

 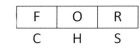 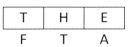

| R E P E N T | F O R | T H E |
| S A L A B F | C H S | F T A |

| K I N G D O M | O F |
| Y U B Z G H D | H C |

| H E A V E N | I S | A T |
| T A W N A B | U K | W F |

| H A N D |
| T W B G |

10. STLMT XT PRCB IMN. (John 20:21)

| P E A C E | B E | W I T H |
| S T L M T | X T | P R C B |

| Y O U |
| I M N |

181

ANSWERS TO CRYPTOGRAMS – SHEET #4

11. KZW BCG DK FZNG Z TZCM HZM. (Psalm 71:5)

Y O U	A R E	M Y	H O P E	O	L O R D
K Z W	B C G	D K	F Z N G	Z	T Z C M

G O D
H Z M

12. ZT KMSC BTDPFY XPBZ BTC GZER LZE TC MY KZZR! (Psalm 136:1)

O H	G I V E	T H A N K S	U N T O	T H E
Z T	K M S C	B T D P F Y	X P B Z	B T C

L O R D	F O R	H E	I S	G O O D
G Z E R	L Z E	T C	M Y	K Z Z R

13. K PSPT K, YB FJP CDEG, YTG HPWKGPW BP FJPEP KW TD WYSKDE. (Is. 43:11)

I	E V E N	I	A M	T H E	L O R D
K	P S P T	K	Y B	F J P	C D E G

A N D	B E S I D E S	M E	T H E R E
Y T G	H P W K G P W	B P	F J P E P

I S	N O	S A V I O R
K W	T D	W Y S K D E

ANSWERS TO CRYPTOGRAMS – SHEET #5

14. P KS BCH WRLJ ZRVL CRWZ RDH, BCH TLHKBRL RI PNLKHW ZRVL MPDO.
(Isaiah 43:15)

I		A	M		T	H	E		L	O	R	D		Y	O	U	R
P		K	S		B	C	H		W	R	L	J		Z	R	V	L

H	O	L	Y		O	N	E		T	H	E		C	R	E	A	T	O	R
C	R	W	Z		R	D	H		B	C	H		T	L	H	K	B	R	L

O	F		I	S	R	A	E	L		Y	O	U	R		K	I	N	G
R	I		P	N	L	K	H	W		Z	R	V	L		M	P	D	O

15. TSK JL FJS JHM PVLP JHM XLLQ TKLLP TKSR MVQ. (Romans 6:7)

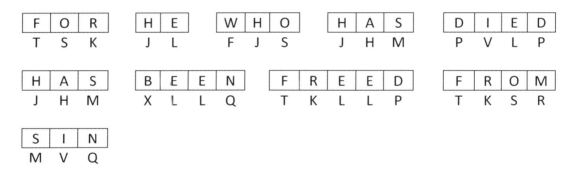

F	O	R		H	E		W	H	O		H	A	S		D	I	E	D
T	S	K		J	L		F	J	S		J	H	M		P	V	L	P

H	A	S		B	E	E	N		F	R	E	E	D		F	R	O	M
J	H	M		X	L	L	Q		T	K	L	L	P		T	K	S	R

S	I	N
M	V	Q

16. BRG HPF BCT VJCKMX'M BRG VJCKMX RM DPG'M. (1 Corinthians 3:23)

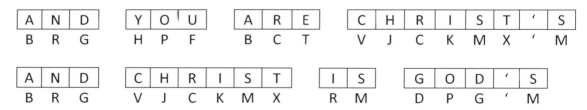

A	N	D		Y	O	U		A	R	E		C	H	R	I	S	T	'	S
B	R	G		H	P	F		B	C	T		V	J	C	K	M	X	'	M

A	N	D		C	H	R	I	S	T		I	S		G	O	D	'	S
B	R	G		V	J	C	K	M	X		R	M		D	P	G	'	M

17. SCW BKTS TCFPP POHW DZ UFOSC. (Romans 1:17)

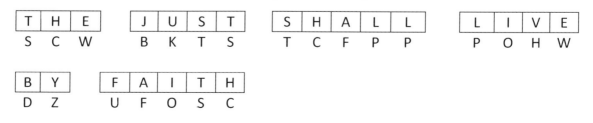

T	H	E		J	U	S	T		S	H	A	L	L		L	I	V	E
S	C	W		B	K	T	S		T	C	F	P	P		P	O	H	W

B	Y		F	A	I	T	H
D	Z		U	F	O	S	C

ANSWERS TO CRYPTOGRAMS – SHEET #6

18. O PE WCY ZBSV PGV WCYSY OJ GB BWCYS; (Isaiah 45:5)

I	A M	T H E	L O R D	A N D
O	P E	W C Y	Z B S V	P G V

T H E R E	I S	N O	O T H E R
W C Y S Y	O J	G B	B W C Y S

19. WHPY C KDSFDPW! (Isaiah 49:13)

S I N G	O	H E A V E N S
W H P Y	C	K D S F D P W

20. UF SVPZGH V FBCWY! (Isaiah 49:13)

B E	J O Y F U L	O	E A R T H
U F	S V P Z G H	V	F B C W Y

21. YZTG, SMLG FH BCFY TGJ MWJ KMPL. (John 5:8)

R I S E	T A K E	U P	Y O U R
Y Z T G	S M L G	F H	B C F Y

B E D	A N D	W A L K
T G J	M W J	K M P L

22. WS WT CLDX KNXTTXY SL MWBX SFGH SL DXRXWBX. (Acts 20:35)

I T	I S	M O R E	B L E S S E D	T O
W S	W T	C L D X	K N X T T X Y	S L

G I V E	T H A N	T O	R E C E I V E
M W B X	S F G H	S L	D X R X W B X

184

ANSWERS TO CRYPTOGRAMS – SHEET #7

23. KMLLSW PMNB CHP WM WVJ GMBU, (Psalm 37:5)

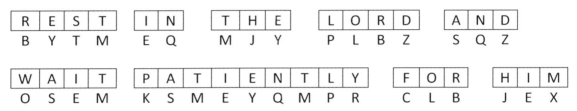

C O M M I T	Y O U R	W A Y	T O	T H E
K M L L S W	P M N B	C H P	W M	W V J

L O R D
G M B U

24. BYTM EQ MJY PLBZ SQZ OSEM KSMEYQMPR CLB JEX (Psalm 37:7)

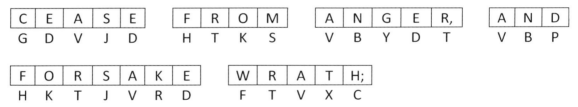

R E S T	I N	T H E	L O R D	A N D
B Y T M	E Q	M J Y	P L B Z	S Q Z

W A I T	P A T I E N T L Y	F O R	H I M
O S E M	K S M E Y Q M P R	C L B	J E X

25. GDVJD HTKS VBYDT VBP HKTJVRD FTVXC; (Psalm 37:8)

C E A S E	F R O M	A N G E R,	A N D
G D V J D	H T K S	V B Y D T	V B P

F O R S A K E	W R A T H;
H K T J V R D	F T V X C

26. YSTEY JL YDK PCSN ZLN NC WCCN; (Psalm 37:3)

T R U S T	I N	T H E	L O R D,	A N D
Y S T E Y	J L	Y D K	P C S N	Z L N

D O	G O O D;
N C	W C C N

27. KRLTML HRQCLPPLP TRPL NY; (Psalm 35:11)

F	I	E	R	C	E
K	R	L	T	M	L

W	I	T	N	E	S	S	E	S
H	R	Q	C	L	P	P	L	P

R	I	S	E
T	R	P	L

U	P;
N	Y

28. KVRTTRF HT PR ZPMTR JBLSTXBRTTHMS HT DMBXHQRS, (Psalm 32:1)

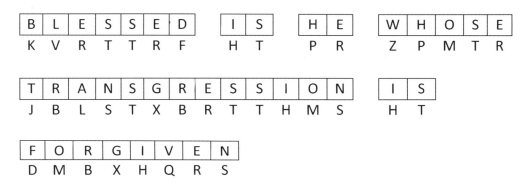

B	L	E	S	S	E	D
K	V	R	T	T	R	F

I	S
H	T

H	E
P	R

W	H	O	S	E
Z	P	M	T	R

T	R	A	N	S	G	R	E	S	S	I	O	N
J	B	L	S	T	X	B	R	T	T	H	M	S

I	S
H	T

F	O	R	G	I	V	E	N
D	M	B	X	H	Q	R	S

29. RTGK ZFSSFNZ ZUTPP LY CF CUY NMDBYX; (Psalm 32:10)

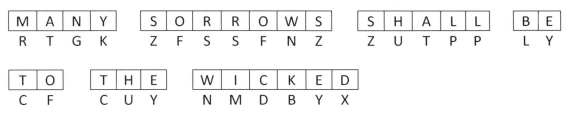

M	A	N	Y
R	T	G	K

S	O	R	R	O	W	S
Z	F	S	S	F	N	Z

S	H	A	L	L
Z	U	T	P	P

B	E
L	Y

T	O
C	F

T	H	E
C	U	Y

W	I	C	K	E	D
N	M	D	B	Y	X

30. HR BW JBBP TBQSYJR (Psalm 31:24)

B	E
H	R

O	F
B	W

G	O	O	D
J	B	B	P

C	O	U	R	A	G	E
T	B	Q	S	Y	J	R

ANSWERS TO CRYPTOGRAMS – SHEET #9

31. SKC DGFVC GK SKC ZGMQ FT GDCM SKC YVSCMT; (Psalm 29:3)

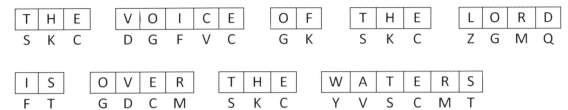

T H E	V O I C E	O F	T H E	L O R D
S K C	D G F V C	G K	S K C	Z G M Q

I S	O V E R	T H E	W A T E R S
F T	G D C M	S K C	Y V S C M T

32. FTBKP YL PDB NWTJ KMJ FTBKPNV PW CB XTKYLBJ (Psalm 48:1)

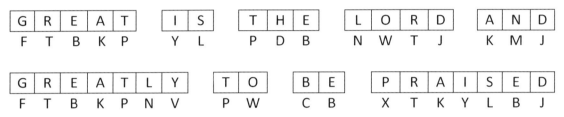

G R E A T	I S	T H E	L O R D	A N D
F T B K P	Y L	P D B	N W T J	K M J

G R E A T L Y	T O	B E	P R A I S E D
F T B K P N V	P W	C B	X T K Y L B J

33. LGR MUKLWP GBUM CSU WXCKGWP (Psalm 47:8)

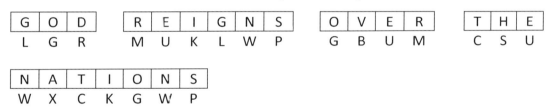

G O D	R E I G N S	O V E R	T H E
L G R	M U K L W P	G B U M	C S U

N A T I O N S
W X C K G W P

34. CW JDRB YWGMPX YC YWB SCTV! (Psalm 105:1)

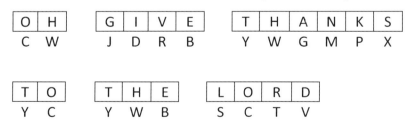

O H	G I V E	T H A N K S
C W	J D R B	Y W G M P X

T O	T H E	L O R D
Y C	Y W B	S C T V

ANSWERS TO CRYPTOGRAMS – SHEET #10

35. TS JTR KPXC N ZPY JPSS HNDD PMYR PY (Eccl. 10:8)

H E	W H O	D I G S	A	P I T	W I L L
T S	J T R	K P X C	N	Z P Y	J P D D

F A L L	I N T O	I T
H N D D	P M Y R	P Y

36. MXDW UVNB FBKXG NZVQ WLK YXWKBD (Eccl. 11:1)

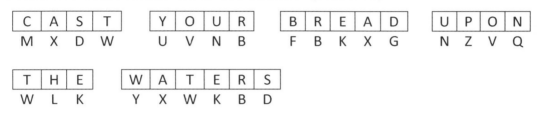

C A S T	Y O U R	B R E A D	U P O N
M X D W	U V N B	F B K X G	N Z V Q

T H E	W A T E R S
W L K	Y X W K B D

37. GTFR USP M BVTN S DSVW; (Psalm 118:25)

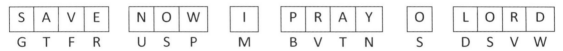

S A V E	N O W	I	P R A Y	O	L O R D
G T F R	U S P	M	B V T N	S	D S V W

38. PUT WSA, LP HUZ C JCNN ARWNX PUT. (Psalm 118:28b)

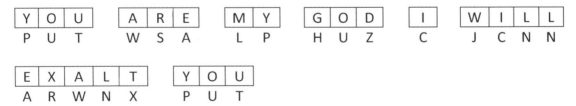

Y O U	A R E	M Y	G O D	I	W I L L
P U T	W S A	L P	H U Z	C	J C N N

E X A L T	Y O U
A R W N X	P U T

39. NETPPTB NT WGT EUKB, (Psalm 124:6)

B L E S S E D	B E	T H E	L O R D
N E T N N T B	N T	W G T	E U K B

40. SMVCQX KPX ZNMF! (Psalm 135:1)

P R A I S E	T H E	L O R D
S M V C Q X	K P X	Z N M F

188

Made in the USA
Middletown, DE
16 May 2024

54379630R00106